AWAKEN THE GENIE WITHIN

A Handbook to Help You Silence
Your Gremlin, Manage Your Emotions and
Bring Out the Best of Who You Are

CONTENTS

INTRODUCTION

Perhaps the greatest gift we can give ourselves is the ability to wake up to our personal truth and live by that truth as often as possible. That is my intention for this book; to offer you some of the insights I share with my coaching clients as well as my own personal experiences from which I continually learn. As you read each passage, I invite you to apply these insights and experiences into your own life for further growth and awakening.

You can read and absorb one page a day or the whole book at once if you need to. No matter how you choose to enjoy this book, you'll learn to recognize when your Genie — your higher self, is being suppressed by your Gremlin.

There are six areas of focus:

"Quieting Your Gremlin" and "Reconnecting With Your Soul"

As you learn to quiet your Gremlin*, you gain greater access to hearing and honoring your Soul's gentle guidance and encouragement. As this unfolds, you are awakening the Genie within**, thereby allowing you to live a life full of wonder and delight.

"Emotional Energy Management" and "Relationships"

These are the two areas where the Gremlin battles furiously with the Genie to maintain its power.

Relationships can bring up many different emotions and depending on how you handle those emotions, you can find your relationships either thriving or struggling. The better you become at managing your emotions for the highest good of all concerned, the sooner you will find yourself in relationships that bring you tremendous joy.

"Changing Your Story" and "Law of Attraction"

More advanced lessons that look at your deeper level issues where your Gremlin can often overtake your Genie.

The Law of Attraction simply states; like energy attracts like energy. The stories you tell yourself, and others, carries a lot of energy. So, it is to your advantage, that you learn to view your experiences with as little drama and negativity as possible. Staying with the facts and not allowing the Gremlin to create more of a story than there really is, awakens the Genie within. This will help you attract what you desire in life.

If you've been introduced to this book by a friend, you'll want to understand a few of my terms used throughout:

The Genie Within** — The gentle, internal voice, or your inherent wisdom who knows your truth, champions you, is your ally and best friend. Your Genie supports you in knocking down your negative thoughts to keep you moving forward. It keeps you present and conscious so you have no need for those past stories that no longer serve you. It wants to come out of the bottle, so to speak, and play or work side-by-side with the universe bringing you all that you desire.

The Gremlin* — The aggressive, internal critic voice, that you have been conditioned to listen to and believe for many years. This voice keeps your fears alive. It believes it is doing you a service by protecting you from making a mistake. The Gremlin is strongly invested in keeping the Genie in the bottle. I have found that naming my Gremlin gives me more power over it and I invite you to do the same. My Gremlin's name is Gertrude.

Vibrational Energy — Science has proven that everything in the universe is made up of energy, including us, and that energy is a vibration. Your energy sends a certain vibration out into the world at all times attracting back to you, your current reality.

Emotional Energy Management — To consciously manage your emotions through your thoughts, words, and feelings, so you attract to you what you do want vs. what you don't want.

I hope you use this book to lift you up when you're feeling down, to bring you clarity during times of confusion, to turn anxiety into peace and fear into confidence.

With Blessings,
Linda

CHAPTER 1

QUIETING YOUR GREMLIN

SELF-HONESTY

I've come to understand that until we are completely honest with ourselves, we will never travel as far down the path to being fully awake as we'd like to believe. We might be able to fool ourselves for the time being, but eventually, we *will* be faced with a similar situation disguised in different clothing that we weren't willing to come clean with earlier on.

For years, while my son was growing up, I volunteered heavily at his school. I'd be in charge of committees only to find myself doing most of the work. I kept telling myself things like, "It isn't a big deal." "The other moms are doing all they can." "I'm just grateful there are people who are willing to do *something*." What I found interesting was when I chose to be the Indian for a while and not the Chief, I still ended up doing most of the work.

It wasn't until I was ready to tell myself the truth that things changed. Very firmly I declared to myself, "It is absolutely not okay that I am doing all this work. I hate this! If someone gets mad at me, then so be it! I'm done." I still remember the feeling I had when I admitted this to myself. I felt so much lighter and empowered. When I expressed my feelings to the other moms they said something that made me laugh inside; "We thought you didn't trust us to do a good job so we backed off and just let you go for it!" Talk about an eye opener!

The fact is, if you want to move through stuff as quickly as possible, then choose self-honesty at every opportunity. The greatest gift you can give yourself and the world is to be honest with yourself and take actions based on your truth.

The key to self-honesty, like anything else that matters to you in life, is your commitment to the process. Because without it, there's only so far you can travel down your path.

I know it can be hard to recognize when you're not being honest with yourself and here are two clues to help you recognize when this is happening: One, you experience an immediate, unsettled feeling. And two, frustration builds up over time. To discover your truth you'll need to search within to see what your Gremlin may be hiding from you. Ask what there is to be gained by being honest with yourself. And, perhaps even more important, ask what you'll lose by not honoring your truth.

All Wrapped Up

When you're all wrapped up in yourself you come in a small package.

Just think about that for a moment. As you wrap your mind around all the issues in your life that you're struggling with or feel overwhelmed by, you keep yourself small. When you're continuously focusing on what's not working in your world it's limiting, stifling, and needless to say, frustrating. This is where your Gremlin wants you to live because this is how it maintains power.

As soon as you allow yourself to look for what *is* working and discover information that can raise your consciousness, you become bigger. You expand. And it's through that expansion that you're no longer so involved with yourself and wrapped up in any past, present and future thoughts that can limit you from being the best you can be.

The next time you're feeling small or less than, imagine unwrapping yourself so you have the mobility to move toward, and attract to you, circumstances, people, and information, that allows you to be all that your soul knows you are meant to be.

PERSPECTIVE IS EVERYTHING

As I sat in my car behind another car, that, for no apparent reason, wasn't moving, my Gremlin was screaming at me to honk my horn. I told her to settle down and give it another few minutes. "No!" she yelled, "There's no good reason the person in front of you should be sitting there so long. You're in a parking lot for crying out loud. They're obviously spacing out!"

Fortunately for me, my Genie thought differently. She told me, "You're only seeing what's happening from one perspective. Relax. The truth will reveal itself."

I decided to be patient, keep my emotions in check, and see what would develop. After about two minutes the car in front of me turned to the left revealing something completely different than what my Gremlin was ranting about.

There was another car that kept the car in front of me from going anywhere. It had stalled and a young man was doing his best to help the driver push the car back into the parking space that the driver had just attempted to pull out of.

Wherever you are physically or emotionally, all you have in the moment is your one perspective. The next time something starts to shift your emotional energy, causing your Gremlin to stand up and shout, imagine there's another perspective ready to reveal itself to you. If it doesn't reveal itself in a timely fashion, then move yourself physically to gain a new perspective or shift your thoughts in the direction of your Genie within.

The more you quiet the Gremlin and awaken the Genie, the better you will be able to manage your emotions.

LIVING LIFE

While flipping through the TV channels preparing to watch one of my favorite shows, a conversation that was taking place between two women on another show, grabbed my attention.

One woman was trying to cheer up her distraught friend and what she said resonated with me. "Lighten up, it's just life! You need to start living it fully, now!" I love that comment, because with the help of our Gremlin, we do make this thing called life into such a bigger deal than it needs to be and we don't live it fully enough most of the time.

After I was uplifted by those words I changed channels to watch my show. During a commercial, I was curious to see if there might be some more great wisdom happening on the other show. I hit the jackpot! The two women I saw earlier were now driving in a convertible, at night, in the pouring rain! They were having a blast hooting and hollering and living life to its fullest.

This reminded me of a conversation I had with a friend about great memories in our life. He shared with me that one of his best memories was when he was seven years old. He and his dad put on their rain gear and rode their bicycles in the rain for an hour, laughing and splashing each other with their bikes. You know what else he said? "That will always be a great day for me because my heart was so full of life."

So what about you? Are you living life as fully as you can? Is there something you want to do but your Gremlin keeps telling you all the reasons why you can't? Today I ask that you drop the reasons why you can't and come up with reasons why you can! Then go make it happen for yourself!

SELF-ACKNOWLEDGMENT

*O*ne of the best obstacles I've ever gotten over was learning how to acknowledge myself for something well done. For as long as I can remember, I always thought it was rude or egotistical to comment, out loud, when I felt good about an accomplishment. At least that's what my Gremlin wanted me to believe!

Well, I'm here to share with you that nothing could be further from the truth. And before I go on, yes, there is a difference between acknowledging yourself for an accomplishment vs. people who brag about how great they are at *everything* they do.

Okay, now that we're clear on that issue here's a few reasons why acknowledging yourself is a good idea:

1. You create an energy within that increases the level of your vibration. This puts you in alignment with attracting more of what you want for yourself.

2. It makes it easier to accept compliments from others. And nothing will turn people off faster than not accepting their compliment. When you don't, it's as if you're telling someone, "Your opinion isn't worthy." "What you have to say is unimportant." Ouch!

And perhaps the most important reason of all:

3. Self-acknowledgment leads to greater self-love. Without self-love it's impossible to really know how to love another.

9

OBSERVING YOUR EGO

The ego is a very powerful thing. And it's the one part of us that can send us reeling and completely keep us from being able to manage our energy, awaken our Genie and most certainly, stop us from quieting the Gremlin. The ego is our Gremlin's best friend.

It can give us a false sense of power and self. It can harm others even if it's not our intention. It can keep us from hearing and listening to what our heart and soul are trying so desperately to tell us.

Over the years I have learned to recognize when my ego's around, and I'm the first to admit, it's an ongoing process keeping it in check — especially during conflicting circumstances with others. The one thing I've recognized though, is when my ego takes over, I have a gut reaction that says, "Stop! Rethink this before you continue." I'm not going to lie to you — sometimes I'm so immersed in ego that I will ignore the warning signs only to suffer the consequences later.

When you begin to step outside of ego some amazing things show up in your life:

1. Love is given and received more easily.

2. Life's roller coaster ride evens out.

3. You become more accepting of others and their opinions and they of you and yours.

4. You take things less personally.

5. You actually hear what others have to say that could be of benefit to you.

6. You stop creating stories around the highs and lows in life, experiencing less drama.

Consider taking a day to observe your ego. Don't judge it. Just watch it and allow it to be an interesting journey of self-discovery. Laugh as often as you can at yourself. Share a mistake you did and turn it into a funny story.

Doing these things brings you a new awareness and the opportunity to step outside of your ego more and more every day.

THE POWER OF BELIEFS

Every one of us has many beliefs. Some of the beliefs we hold can truly catapult us to reach our desires while other beliefs do nothing but keep us receiving what we don't want over and over again.

A very wise man by the name of Robert Bolton once said:

A belief is not merely an idea the mind possesses;
it is an idea that possesses the mind.

When the mind is possessed by your Gremlin's beliefs, you are guaranteed results that are less than satisfying. However, when the mind is focused on your Genie's beliefs, you are guaranteed results of great satisfaction.

It's so important to keep checking in with yourself around your beliefs. Make note of the ones that you've brought with you from your younger years. And if those beliefs aren't serving your highest good now, then check again to see if that's actually your belief or someone's belief from your past that you took on and brought into the present.

The more you revisit your beliefs, the more you give yourself the opportunity to eliminate those that don't really belong to you and replace them with beliefs that are connected to your heart and soul in the here and now.

Do not underestimate the power of a belief. It will deliver you a life of expansion or a life of limitation every time.

GROWTH OVER TIME

Considering how many years your Gremlin thoughts have been around, it's always interesting to me how people expect immediate results to turn those thoughts into thoughts that are more Genie-like.

Think about it for a second; if your Gremlin's been in charge for twenty to fifty years, or longer, then it shouldn't be a surprise if it takes an entire year to quiet your Gremlin enough so you can experience your Genie thoughts on a more regular basis.

Like anything in life, change is a process. It takes time and patience to grow into your Genie thinking. And the time it takes is so worth the wait because the life you experience with this kind of thinking is truly one of tremendous joy.

There's a certain bamboo plant that needs watering and nurturing every day to survive. It will grow about a foot in the first year and then as it's cared for everyday for the next few years, there's no sign of growth.

But suddenly, just when you think it will no longer grow, it grows to 90 FEET in its fourth year!

Now here's the key to this growth — if you stop caring for it before the growth spurt, it will die and you'll have to start all over again with a new plant. The real shame is that you never really knew just how close you might have been to witnessing that growth spurt.

So like the bamboo plant, you must nurture your Genie thinking every single day so it can grow to its full potential and prove to you how capable it is in quieting your Gremlin and be the one who's in charge most of the time.

Natural Healing Process

Rose bushes 1, Linda 0. That's the score that took place while I was out in my garden trimming my roses. Thinking about all sorts of things that I needed to get done except what was in front of me in the moment, I lost my footing and went flailing into the rose bushes. Ouch!

Wearing a pair of shorts and a sleeveless shirt, you can imagine what I looked like when I was able to stand back up — thorns tearing my body, scratches all over my legs and arms, with enough blood to have me running into the house to clean up the mess. Oh yeah, a little swelling in certain areas from the toxins. Just lovely.

When I was cleaned up, I went back out to finish the job, only this time with great attention and care — allowing for a more pleasant experience.

Over the next few days I watched the healing process that took place throughout my body. Nothing short of miraculous! In just a few days the scratches diminished tremendously, the swelling disappeared and the tenderness was completely gone.

The body doesn't need to quiet any Gremlin or manage its emotional energy in order to heal. It already knows, beyond a shadow of a doubt, the healing will happen. And, our body certainly doesn't have to reconnect with the soul to start the healing process because there was never a disconnect to begin with. The connection to Spirit is always there when healing is taking place.

When we don't let our Gremlin take over our mind about what happened and why it happened, all healing can take place in a miraculously short period of time.

So the next time you find yourself needing to heal emotionally, do your best to quiet your Gremlin and let your Genie and Divine guidance assist you in speeding up the natural healing process that is always available to you.

WHAT'S ON YOUR LINE

Sometimes when I'm on my home phone there's static on the line. This particular day was one of those times. During the entire call I was tolerating the static and it was quite annoying, especially since I've changed phones and played with the wiring on several occasions. When I got off the call I found myself in a low energy place because of it. Within a matter of seconds a thought came to me that this low energy is exactly what happens to us when there's static on our spiritual line.

Static on your spiritual line comes in the form of fear, worry, anxiety, anger, frustration, and so on. When the static is there it's very difficult to receive information clearly and easily; such as an inspired idea or the ability to feel gratitude for the little things in life. Static is more than just noise; it actually means having no motion.

When there's static on your line just remember it's your Gremlin messing with your internal wiring. Simply go about the process of quieting it down so you can clear the line for your Genie to get through, raising your energy and getting you back into motion.

KNOWLEDGE IS POWER...OR IS IT?

We gain a lot of knowledge in our life as we continue to study and learn into our adult lives. And supposedly, with that knowledge, comes some power. As the saying goes, knowledge is power. Or is it?

The way I see it, there are a lot of people in the world who are collecting quite a bit of knowledge to help them with their spiritual growth but don't necessarily put it to use. And when you don't put to use the knowledge you've gained, what good is it?

If you're going to put in the effort to learn new things that can help you expand your consciousness and way of being in life, then you've got to put what you know to use. Yes, I realize this sounds incredibly obvious and maybe you're wondering why I would write about the obvious?

The answer is simple. I've lost count of the number of people I've talked to over the years about all the knowledge they've gained to better their lives and yet year in and year out, there are little, if any, real profound growth changes that take place.

Are you someone who is gaining knowledge around your spiritual awareness but not really finding yourself any happier? Are you learning things one day only to find yourself not practicing over time what you've learned? If you answered yes to these questions then be willing to dig a little deeper and discover why this is so for you.

The reasons can vary from person to person. For some people the fear of change is stronger than the desire for change so no action is taken. If this is so for you, you may discover that you need to reach utter misery to make your desire for change stronger than your fear. When this happens you no longer let the fear stop you from growing emotionally and spiritually.

If you prefer *not* to hit bottom, then take baby steps to create the change even with the fear there. The only real way to eliminate fear is to move through it. As you do, you will find yourself gaining greater courage along the way and more willing to take bigger steps. Remember, fear comes from the stories your Gremlin tells you. You have no idea how something will be until you are living it. Your past doesn't equal the future so let the past go and start from right where you are.

If your inability to apply what you've learned stems from laziness — wanting to experience change, but not willing to do the work involved — then all the knowledge you obtain won't do much good. Again, you've got to *want* to create change more than you don't want to. When you're comfortable in your life, it's easy to sit back and do nothing with the information even though, deep down, you know there's something more you want for your life. Sometimes asking someone to support you through your journey is all that it may take to shake off the laziness and take some action. It can help to be held accountable by someone you trust when your heart truly wants something but your Gremlin is telling you to take another nap in the hammock.

I invite you to honestly check-in with yourself to discover what holds you back from not applying what you're learning. When you have your answer, your new awareness brings you that much closer to turning your knowledge into a deeper spiritual awakening.

COMPARISON, THE
SELF-INFLICTED PAIN

Perhaps one of the greatest ways we bring pain onto ourselves is through comparing anything and everything in our life with someone else's life. Whether it's a job, physical appearance, finances, children and whatever else you can think of that you find yourself comparing from time to time.

What is there to be gained from comparing your life situation with someone else? If we look at this from both ends of the spectrum, either way it's lose/lose.

Perhaps you compare yourself to someone in this way, "Hey, I'm in great shape compared to that fat person." Or, "Wow, compared to that homeless person, I've got it made!"

That may appear to have a positive spin on it but it doesn't. Why? Because your Gremlin is just as involved in the positive comparison for yourself as the negative.

The Gremlin says, "As long as there's someone who has it worse off than me, then I'm okay." But the minute you see someone else who you're envious of in some way, you're now thrown to the other side of the spectrum feeling inadequate about your circumstances. The result? You've become a human yo yo — up, down, up down.

When you come from your soul, comparison isn't even a consideration because your soul already knows you're exactly as you need to be in the moment. And so is every other person.

If you choose to make some changes because you *want* to and not because of some external comparison, great! If not, that's perfect too!

Watch yourself as you move through the day and see where your Gremlin has you playing the comparison game and the kind of emotional energy that it creates for you.

STOP THE WAR!

No, not that war! The other war. The war that you're much more intimately involved with and that you actually have the power to do something about. The internal war. This war consists of self-judgment, indecisiveness, comparisons, feelings of being inadequate, believing that you shouldn't be where you are in life and anything else you fight about with yourself over and over again.

The sooner you wake up to the notion that there's a war going on within you — or whenever you step into your Gremlin thinking — the sooner you can make peace with yourself and start allowing for the possibility that you're perfect just as you are and exactly where you need to be in life at this moment.

For a long time I would allow myself to get so angry with drivers who cut me off on the freeway. And I got cut off a lot! I'd lean on my horn, and occasionally, I'd race up to the driver just to stare him or her down. Of course he or she never noticed *me*, which drove me even more nuts. And on top of that, I was upset for hours after the incident.

When I started learning about the ideas behind the Universal Laws, I had an awakening with my freeway experiences. The only war that was going on was inside of me and I had complete control in stopping this war. I made a vow that the next time people cut me off, I would bless them to arrive safely and send them on their way. Interestingly enough, within a matter of days, no one was cutting me off anymore.

Embracing, instead of fighting one's reality, keeps you attuned to the natural evolution of your life's journey. Every time you struggle to fight off what you don't want in your life, the more you're inviting it into your life because of the attention you give it. When you misplace your energy and attention, only a circumstance with that same energy can keep showing up.

Stop the war by choosing, from a peaceful consciousness, where you want to be next or how you want to experience your life. From there, move into a state of knowing before it actually manifests in solid form, by feeling what it would be like to already be in that experience.

Authenticity and You

The dictionary defines authentic as; Worthy of trust, reliance or belief. Genuine.

When I apply the word authentic to people in my life I describe them as people I can count on, who are a joy to be with because I know what to expect from them. They don't live from a hidden agenda and they inspire me to be my best authentic self as well.

As nice as that sounds it's not always easy for people to live consistently in a place of authenticity. When you get right down to it, authenticity is about trusting yourself above all else. It's about being comfortable enough to show your true self to others without concern of what they may think of you.

There are a few advantages to trusting yourself enough to be fully authentic. The more you do, the more you attract authentic people to you. Your authenticity radar holds a greater awareness to recognize those who aren't living from their authenticity. And perhaps the best advantage of all, you don't have to keep changing your Beingness depending on whom you're with. Now that's exhausting!

When you're the real deal, people who are in alignment with that vibration will show up and add joy to your life. While the others will come and go with little fanfare. Your authenticity allows for more peace and truth to be experienced on a daily basis.

More and more I am experiencing the desire of those I coach who want to remove their mask and reveal their authentic self.

I have to admit, nothing brings me more joy than when clients step onto that path of their life. And, the best part is, *they* start experiencing more personal freedom and joy when they do this. Talk about win/win!

I'd like to ask you some questions. Do you feel successful on the outside but like a fraud on the inside? Is your public face a mask that portrays strength but underneath is fear? Are there people in your life who drain you? Do you make decisions based upon what others think or want, just to be accepted?

Your authentic self is that place, deep within, that has the answers to these questions. This is where your truths, beliefs, values and dreams live. It's here that you know how you really feel even though you may be uncomfortable admitting it to the world or even to yourself, at times.

If you've been living everyone else's life and putting yours on the back burner, it's never too late to awaken your authentic self and listen closely as the truth is whispered to you. This takes courage. It means being willing to say no when you might normally say yes if your yes isn't authentic.

Give yourself a gift today. Let go of your "have to" and "should" for a little while. Slow down, listen to what your heart is telling you. What do you hear? Look inside. Who do you see?

When you start to see a glimmer of your authentic self, embrace it and allow it to flow to the surface. Then take the steps that are needed to support this part of you as you reveal it to the world. Remember, it's the infinitesimal steps that can create the biggest transformation.

> *The most common despair is...not choosing, or willing, to be oneself, but the deepest form of despair is to choose to be other than oneself.*
> ~ SOREN KIERKEGAARD — 19TH CENTURY
> DANISH PHILOSOPHER

LOOK UP. WAY UP!

⌒

During my walk, I did what I often do when I'm walking up a big, long hill. I put my head down and just focus on the small area of pavement directly in front of me. When I look too far ahead I start to feel less energetic, as if I'm not going to make it to the top and I want to turn around.

Well, during this particular walk I experienced something very different. With my head down and plodding along, a little voice in me said, "Look up. Way up!" So I did, and what a difference it made.

I saw an expansive, beautiful blue sky with magnificent clouds and lush, rich green trees with the sun's rays shining through them. I felt so connected to my surroundings that it brought tears to my eyes. It was as though my entire Being was opening up and I found myself both energized and grateful for listening to that gentle, kind voice within.

Many times we put our heads down with our nose to the grindstone so we can do exactly what we need to do in order to accomplish a goal. As practical and helpful as this can be to keep us moving forward, it can also be limiting, shortsighted and all encompassing. When we're willing to take a moment to look up, way up, we can see the bigger picture and gain greater insights. We're given a new perspective that can leave us feeling elated and renewed, giving us even more momentum to keep on going.

Wow!

I saw a commercial that showed various vignettes of people seeing something and simply saying, "Wow!" Some wows were full of excitement. Some were more quiet and awe like. While some exuded joy and laughter.

When the commercial ended, my first thought was how great it would be to allow ourselves to find something every day to be wowed by. And then my next thought, which I credit my Gremlin, Gertrude for, was there probably isn't something to be wowed by *every* day.

Well, when Gertrude shows up like that, I choose to challenge her. So I decided to find something to be wowed by every single day for as long as possible. And you know what? Taking on this little experiment proved to me that there is something to say "Wow!" to each day. And all of these wows do run the gamut of total excitement to a state of quiet awe. The best part of this experiment is the fact that it's become a part of my day-to-day experience and I find myself attracting more and more things to be wowed by that I may have never noticed before.

Here are a few "Wow!" experiences I've had: Standing in an open field, a feather floated down in front of me with no bird in sight! There was a hawk sitting on a tree in front of my house. A person driving a 2-wheel car with a clear bubble top was driving next to me.

What's the advantage of noticing these wow things? It lifts your spirit and raises your vibration! And when your vibration is raised...Well, I think you know the rest of that thought!

So starting today, I invite you to move through all of your days looking for things to be able to say "Wow!" to.

BUILDING YOUR
SPIRITUAL MUSCLES

E verybody knows that the best way to strengthen physical muscles is by using them. You've got lots of different muscles and depending on which ones you feel need more strength, those will be the ones you tend to focus on and build up.

If you want stronger arms you work on your biceps. For a stronger stomach, abs. Mid thigh, your quads and of course there's always the "favorite" of so many women, the buttocks, which means working on the gluteus maximus.

Without the effort there are not many changes that are going to take place. Interestingly enough, the same is true when building a different set of muscles. The problem is, most people aren't as willing to put in the effort, even though they really *want* to experience the change with these muscles. I'm talking about your spiritual muscles. Those would be your courage, authenticity, self-esteem, truth, compassion, forgiveness, self-love, non-judgments and patience, to name a few.

If some of those muscles are weak for you, then it's worth finding a source of support to make them stronger. When building physical strength, the gym or personal trainer is often a source of support. The support for your spiritual muscles may be reading inspirational material, listening to motivational tapes, hiring a life coach, meditating, going on a retreat or meeting regularly with a group of spiritually minded people. Whatever it is, it needs to feel right for you, because if it doesn't, you won't stick with it — just like anything else you're not in alignment with.

Building both sets of muscles requires your desire, commitment and consistency. Without those ingredients, it's too easy to quit before you've experienced any real change.

WHAT KIND OF AN ADDICT ARE YOU?

I don't suppose that's a question you've been asked a lot over your lifetime or one that you would even associate yourself with.

You see, most people relate the word addict to things like, drugs, alcohol, food or even sex. These are the more obvious addictions. But there are other types of addictions that I'd like to bring to your attention. You may not think of them as addictions but even so, consider the possibility. Some serve our highest good and others, well...not so much.

For instance, I'm addicted to things like joy, inspirational books, laughter, gratitude, inner peace and silence. After reading that, you may decide you're someone who's addicted to these kinds of things, too! Because of these addictions, my life gets better and better and I would imagine yours does, too.

Now with that said, there are other types of addictions that many people in the world live with. The need to please others, complaining, jealousy, gossip, being judgmental, pretending to always be happy, controlling, worry, illness or playing the victim. Those are just off the top of my head but I think it's enough to get your attention. And, they are all addictions your Gremlin thrives on.

Take a moment to get quiet inside and then be honest with yourself before you answer these questions:

1. Do you spend more time than you would like to with any of those behaviors?

2. Do you find yourself unable to stop even when you say you'll no longer engage in a particular behavior?

If you said yes, then you're on the road to recovery. The first step is to always tell yourself the truth. The next step is to consider how your life would be improved without any of those addictions. And the third step is to seek out ways to assist you in kicking the habit(s) so you can participate in addictions that bring you more happiness!

CHAPTER 2

RECONNECTING WITH YOUR SOUL

STAYING THE SPIRITUAL COURSE

I often receive emails from people asking me how to stay the course of their spiritual growth. They'll say things like; "With all that's happening in the world, it's so hard to stay focused." Or, "How can I feel happy when there's so much pain out there?"

The more you focus on everything that isn't working, the more you continue to attract that into your life and then you aren't doing yourself, or the world, any good. The world needs you to start from the inside and work your way out. It needs you to be responsible in finding your own peace and joy so your good energy can spread to others and become part of the process for shifting the world's energy.

> *We are all like voyagers in a distant city. We came from the world of Spirit to a world that has lost sight of its origin and purpose. It is easy to become distracted by fears and illusions and to forget who we are and why we came.*
>
> ~ ALAN COHEN

It's up to you to decide what's going to reconnect you with your soul — to help you remember who you are and why you're here, so you *do* stay on track. And, what's crucial, is that you do whatever serves you best. That which feels good! When you feel good, your vibration is raised and that vibration reaches the universe creating the reality you desire.

1. Listen to music that feeds your soul.

2. Spend time with spiritually alive friends.

3. Read inspiring books regularly.

4. Keep a gratitude journal.

5. Take time to meditate/pray.

6. Dance.

7. Walk in nature.

8. Work with someone to keep expanding your consciousness.

9. Keep a journal of favorite quotes and read it often.

10. Exercise regularly.

Perhaps some, or all of these suggestions feel good to you. Either way, stay close to your heart as you continue on your path, and I promise you, little by little, change will take place internally and externally.

LAUGHTER FOR THE SOUL

Do you think you laugh a lot? I certainly thought I did, until I read an article about laughter and boy do I have some catching up to do. The study showed that out of one thousand adults, 40% didn't laugh at all during the week and the other 40% laughed up to eighty-nine times a day. (I have no idea what happened to the other 20%!)

Eighty-nine times a day seemed like a lot to me until the study revealed that five-year old children laugh up to four hundred times a day! Wow! We tend to be so serious as we grow up. Yes, there's a lot going on in life with responsibilities and problems to solve, but does that mean the laughter has to stop?

Absolutely not!

When you make a choice to lighten up and laugh more, you break through repetitive thought patterns that keep you stuck. Laughter boosts your immune system, tones and relaxes muscles, lessens anxiety and depression and helps you be more creative and productive. You experience more joy, which raises your vibration and helps you attract more of what you want in life.

Why not make a conscious decision this week to laugh as often as possible and notice how you feel and what you attract into your life that is more to your liking. There's nothing your soul loves more than a good laugh!

As for me, I'm going to find some five year olds to hang out with and laugh the day away!

THE SOUL'S TIMING

In the New Testament the Greeks used two words to represent time; chronos and kairos.

Chronos means time based on hours, minutes and seconds. Kairos represents the right moment, perfect timing.

It is kairos that your soul understands above all else. A knowingness that there is a Divine order to all that is taking place in life. As you move toward reconnecting with your soul, you will find the guidance within to TRUST — allowing you to Totally Rely Upon Spirit's Timing.

If you're working on a project or want to create a new career, only to find yourself frustrated with the pace things are moving at, shift your attention away from chronos and toward kairos. When you've done the groundwork give yourself permission to hang back for a little bit. Create an opening for the universe to have its turn at doing what it does best, filling the space with what you need next to move you a little closer to your ultimate desire.

IN SEARCH OF APPROVAL

How often do you find yourself unable to move forward with certain dreams because you're waiting to receive approval from other people in your life? Here's the bottom line on approval:

You will never, ever, a million times over get everyone's approval.

When I decided to spend less time working in my lucrative career in the film industry to pursue my coaching, writing and speaking dream, there were many more people telling me why it was a bad idea than those who said, "Go for it!" I knew those who weren't approving of this change couldn't imagine taking a risk like this for themselves. The feelings they expressed were about their fears, not mine.

Some of the biggest movers and shakers in our history — like Martin Luther King, Golda Meir, Ghandi, Nelson Mandela — for example, had a difficult time getting people to not only approve of their plans, dreams, or beliefs, but they were faced with many people who didn't like them. And fortunately for the world, that didn't stop them.

When there's a strong enough pull for you to move forward with something your heart and soul are guiding you toward, go for it. Forget about being admired by others. Forget about being accepted. Forget about being liked. All of that concern comes from your Gremlin because it needs fuel for the fire.

When you're connected to your Genie within, the need for others' approval falls away so you're free to pursue what makes you most happy. The only place approval needs to come from is you.

So, what have you been holding back from accomplishing in your life, because of lack of approval or fear?

BUSY SOUL

Are you one of those people who's always busy? Rushing here and there. Gotta go do this and finish that. If you are, you might want to slow down for a moment and consider if your busyness is feeding your soul or starving it.

The more you're able to say no, the more time you'll have to feed your soul. Why not give yourself a fresh start, beginning now, by observing yourself throughout the next few days and determine a few things:

1. Are you feeling energized with your busyness or depleted?

If you're energized that's great! This means you feel good about what you're doing, even if it's the everyday tasks that need to get done. And, it's also an indication that you're living a balanced life.

Now, if you're depleted, you need to step back and really consider how much you're taking on throughout your day and what you're agreeing to that you don't need to. This is where learning to say no can really help. Consider letting go of the need to be in control of everything and start delegating. It doesn't matter how many times you've gotten a no in the past when asking for help. Keep asking and let people know how much it would mean to you.

Notice how you're asking for help. Is it in a way that assumes you'll be turned down? Is there annoyance in your voice? Or, do you hold the intention that someone will step up to the plate for you? And the biggest question of all is, are you willing to let go of being in total control to receive the help you need?

2. Are you staying busy so you don't have to feel something or face a situation?

The problem with this is that all your running around is really about running away. Situations that you're stressed out about don't always just disappear when ignored and will eventually need to be addressed. Feelings can only be pushed down so far until there's no more room to push them and then WHAM, they come rushing up to the surface needing emergency attention. The sooner you're willing to slow down and face whatever you're avoiding, the sooner your stress will leave, your energy will return, and your soul will be fed.

3. Do you find yourself getting impatient easily?

This is a strong indication you're overloaded and need to replenish your soul. When you take care of yourself, not only do you win, but everyone around you wins. When you're rested, your patience level goes way up and your relationships improve.

Do something for yourself every day that makes you happy. It doesn't have to be huge. Even just sitting and sipping your favorite cup of tea while listening to soothing music can feed your soul enough to give you the extra energy and patience you need. If you've got a cat or dog, taking time to pet them can relax you. There are no steadfast rules here. You know better than anyone what brings you enough joy to help you relax and feed your soul. The key here is making yourself the priority for a change!

4. Is your health affected in some way?

This is another sure-fire way to determine if you've taken on too much and you're depleting your soul. It's crucial to listen to your body. It doesn't lie and is really good at conspiring with your soul to get you to slow down for a while by bringing on physical symptoms that can take you down for the count.

Don't mask the symptoms with drugs, legal or illegal. Nourish your body and soul with good nutrition and rest. Spend time with friends, your kids, or in recreation. Your soul is screaming out to you for this care. I know you're already aware of this, but it pays to be reminded because in our busyness, we tend to look for a quick fix or ignore the signs altogether, instead of honoring what's going to serve us in the long run.

STAYING TRUE TO YOURSELF

Staying true to yourself and your spiritual growth can be challenging when those you're close to are not on the same page as you are.

As you experience wonderful, new insights, that make a huge difference in your life, it's normal to want to share everything you've been learning with those who are struggling in their life, with the hopes of helping them.

When someone you know is making choices that are leading him down a path that can bring him great pain, it's natural to want to step in and stop him from continuing down this path. However, he may not be ready to hear what you have to say and that path may be exactly where he needs to be in order to ultimately discover the right path for himself.

This doesn't mean you can't be true to yourself by expressing your concerns and gently share some insights that might help. The key, however, is to be willing to say what you believe is true and have no attachment to his response or ultimate decision.

Part of your spiritual growth is the ability to recognize your truth, embrace it fully, reveal it to others with confidence and respect, while maintaining your compassion, when those you care about still choose to continue on a path that isn't necessarily serving their highest good or one you would not choose for yourself.

Slowly Speeding Forward Step by Step

A client expressed to me that she wanted more to do during the week between our sessions so the changes she desired could happen more quickly.

Although this sounds like a logical way to go about creating change for yourself, it can often be the exact way to set you back rather than move you forward. When you've finally committed to the journey necessary to create change in your life, it's a very exciting time and quite normal to want to speed forward.

The problem is, when you attempt to speed forward without really taking the time to connect deeply with everything you're learning, you'll find yourself standing on a foundation with a lot of cracks in it. And the minute you hit a speed bump, what you built up to that point would come tumbling down faster than ever before.

Patience is such a mandatory part of your growing process. The more you try to force something to happen sooner than it's naturally ready to, the less prepared you are for greater growth and results.

It's wonderful to be excited about the next step and then the next. I encourage that above all else. Just make sure before you move onto the next step, that the one before is on solid ground. Life isn't a race. Wherever you are on your path is exactly where you're meant to be or you wouldn't be there.

BEING READY TO CONTRIBUTE

Occasionally I'm asked about how much to tithe either through money or time. My answer is quite simple:

Until you are truly in a place of being ready to contribute something, whether it's money or your time, don't do anything. Why? Because giving out of obligation creates more internal upset than relief.

I know there are tons of people out there who would chew my head off for this comment, but the bottom line, in my humble opinion, is we need to feel good about the contributions we make toward any cause we give to.

If your contribution is done out of fear or guilt, then you are not giving from the purity of your heart. There is no joy when contributing in this way. Everyone's circumstances are different and therefore not everyone will be ready to give back in ways that others believe they should.

When you feel ready in your heart to contribute in a way that feels right for you, your contribution will have a much greater impact on both the giver and the receiver.

ALIGNMENT WITH OUR NATURAL FLOW

A dear friend gave me a little water fountain for my office, which I just love. The sound of flowing water always soothes my soul.

After putting it together, filling it with water and then turning it on, I was surprised at the amount of water spilling out beyond the fountain and onto my desk. Quickly turning it off, I stared at it for a moment not understanding what I had done wrong.

I placed a container under it so I could turn it on again and observe it a bit longer. What I realized was quite wonderful because it was such a perfect representation of what happens to us in life.

The pieces were out of alignment — the rocks and the platforms holding the rocks. Once I adjusted the platforms and some of the rocks, I tried again. This time less watered spilled over, but still not perfect. I took a closer look and saw the main obstacle that stopped the gentle flow of the water and shifted it. Eureka! The fountain was on and the water flowed easily over the rocks leaving me with a feeling of peace and satisfaction.

Just like this fountain, when we're out of emotional alignment, the negative energy we're experiencing will spill over taking us out of the flow of life. In those moments it's necessary to turn off the emotion long enough to notice what obstacles are causing the misalignment.

The answer may not reveal itself the first time we try or even the second or third time, but when we keep looking inside and observing in earnest, the answer is always there. And in that moment, we have the opportunity to make the adjustments necessary, allowing us to be in alignment with our natural flow once again.

EXPERIENCES UNTO THEMSELVES

Many years ago I was on a spiritual retreat. During one of the evening meditations I experienced a deep connection to everything in the universe. There was no separation at all. I felt what it was like being free of a body and just being total energy. It was extremely powerful.

When I came out of my meditation, the others in the room were sitting patiently as they had already completed their meditation. I shared my experience the best I knew how, but as always, with profound experiences, words could not truly capture the essence of the experience.

The next evening we went into another meditation. Although I did my best to relax and let go, I felt myself striving to relive the meditation from the night before. Not surprisingly, I was the one waiting for everyone else to finish their meditation that night. To say I was disappointed is an understatement.

Today, I am more grateful for the meditation I struggled with because of the lessons I received. I learned that each experience in life is not meant to be compared. When we can accept whatever is happening in a particular experience we will find ourselves much more at peace. To strive to repeat a joyful experience is futile and can lead to great frustration.

When we live our life moment to moment and don't bring along other past moments, it frees us up to truly experience and accept the moment we're in. The more fully we experience and accept that moment, the more there is to be gained by it. And this is true for an experience that brings us pleasure or one that is temporarily unpleasant.

A Divine Spirit

When my son, Kyle, was eighteen years old and preparing to leave for a two month trip through Europe, to be followed up by a quick week home and then off to college, I was feeling nostalgic. His days of living at home full time were coming to an end and it had me revisiting the last eighteen years in my mind. One event stands out above all else.

When he was four years old he was playing with his six year old friend and neighbor, Danny. There were two police officers in the neighborhood for reasons I don't recall. When they left, Danny said to Kyle, "Did you see how tall that black policeman was? He was huuuuuge!"

Kyle's response? "What black policeman? They were dressed in blue!"

In that moment I saw the way my four year old viewed the world and I desperately wanted to freeze time and always have it be like that for him; seeing people beyond the color of their skin, the shape of their eyes or anything else that makes us look different from each other. A thought that didn't even enter his consciousness.

It was such a profound opportunity to fully recognize that we are not born with any preconceived notions, ideas or prejudices. How we see the world and the beliefs we hold are all learned. And if that's true, then that means anything we don't like about ourselves in regard to our choices, behaviors or thinking, can be changed, allowing ourselves to reconnect to the Divine Spirit within.

JUDGMENT

~~~

One of the spiritual practices that I play with as consistently as possible in my life is letting go of judgment. Do I always succeed? Absolutely not! Am I getting better and better at it? Absolutely yes!

And with that said, when I found myself judging something that I was reading and making the writer's comments wrong, I could literally feel my energy drain and my vibration start to lower. Then it hit me like a lightening bolt! Every time I judge someone I'm draining my own life force. I'm stripping myself of peace and joy. I'm hurting myself!

With this new awareness, I chose to read the article again from a place of neutrality. Letting the words be there without making them right or wrong. What a freeing experience it was! I not only felt my joy return but I found myself interested in another's opinion, learning something new, without feeling like I had to defend my belief or make the writer wrong for his belief.

It's clear to me now, that every judgment, no matter how big or small, has a price. And the price can be pretty big when it comes to our own happiness and ability to move further down our spiritual path.

WHAT WOULD LOVE DO NOW?

Sometimes life gets messy. Sometimes life can leave us feeling like we'll never fully get it. Sometimes there are just no easy choices and yet a choice still has to be made.

In those moments of messiness, not getting it, or tough choices, ask yourself, "What would love do now?" These five simple words can truly transform your thinking and actions in ways that can take you further along your spiritual path more rapidly than you might imagine. As human beings we complicate things greatly, and in our quest to be the best we can be, this is the one question that allows us to be just that.

Even in the most frustrating or painful situations, "What would love do now?" assists you in seeing things from a higher perspective so you're able to guide yourself in a direction that leaves you feeling at peace with your choices.

LISTEN TO CREATE A
QUIET MIND

While sleeping soundly one night, I was woken up abruptly by a loud noise. As I lay there very still, listening intently to figure out what it was I heard, I noticed something after a few minutes. My mind was absolutely quiet the entire time. No thoughts whatsoever. Of course, once I realized this, my mind was no longer quiet but it was a wonderful awareness in the moment.

I decided to do an experiment. For the entire day, any chance I had, I just listened to the sounds that existed. The sound of my steps as I walked across a room. The running water. Doors opening and closing. Light switches being turned on and off. The faint sounds in the distance outside. The sound of the computer keypad. The birds, wind, cars, dogs, children laughing. Whatever I was doing, wherever I went, if the opportunity allowed me to just listen to the various sounds around me, I did. Every time I did this, my mind was silent. There was no identification as to what the sound was. Just awareness.

By the end of the day I found myself more relaxed and at peace than I normally am. My day was free of thoughts about the past and worries about the future. It was a profound experience and one that I encourage you to try for yourself. If you notice yourself identifying what you're hearing, quickly bring your attention back to your listening. Consider this a moving meditation for an entire day.

INTEGRATE AT A
SOUL LEVEL, *THEN* SHARE
WITH OTHERS

W hen I first started coaching, I found myself sharing with my clients, many of the things I just learned if I thought it could help them with their situation. Although my intention was always for the highest purpose, I would become frustrated when the clients wouldn't embrace the learning the way I had. I needed them to get it! What a grave disservice I did to them *and* myself.

When I shared this with my mentor at the time, she said one word, three times, that made perfect sense to me. Integrate, integrate, integrate. You see, although I had grasped my new learning at an intellectual level, I didn't give it the time and nurturing it deserved to reach me at my soul's level. I needed to allow the information to birth through me before I gave it away to others. By giving it away too quickly, I saw that I was easily effected by others' responses to my sharing because it wasn't a strong enough belief in my own Being. I would doubt myself and then allow myself to get dragged into their story or drama more deeply.

Here's what I now know: Most of the time when we learn something that creates a shift in us it can often take time for it to reach us at a soul level. You may not realize it in the moment because it's so exciting to experience the aha's. And, with that said, it's at the level of your soul's knowing, when you can confidently and easily share what you've learned, to help others, without needing them to agree with you or try it on for themselves. You share because it feels right and whatever follows is absolutely perfect.

SOMETIMES IT'S A PAINFUL AND BUMPY JOURNEY

Throughout the years of waking myself up to a higher consciousness, there have been times when I found it difficult to get out of bed. Choosing to lie there and cry my eyes out. Not talk to anyone. Not go anywhere. My heart and soul hurt so badly that I just wanted to go to sleep and not wake up again until the feeling was gone.

What I've come to understand about these moments is that they are absolutely a necessary part of our spiritual growth. It's an opportunity to recognize that something is trying to emerge through us, break through, so we not only have a greater understanding of what we've experienced up to that point in life, but so we can apply that understanding into our lives to achieve more of our heart's desires and be even more awake than before.

I guess you could say we're not that much different from a caterpillar who goes through the necessary stages to emerge into a beautiful butterfly. It may start out slow and arduous, but as it grows in size and strength, it's ready for its next stage of life. One that consists of a resting period so when it emerges into that butterfly, it's ready to spread its wings and reveal its beauty to the world as it was always meant to do.

I encourage you to embrace your resting periods with self-love, patience and gentleness as you prepare your new wings to carry you to even higher places than ever before.

THE RECIPE OF LIFE

Since cooking is not one of my favorite things to do in the world, I was rather surprised when an analogy came to me about cooking recipes and the recipe of life. Before I go any further I do want to say, I'm not a bad cook, it's just that I don't get tremendous joy from the whole process. Now with that said, there are certain recipes I truly enjoy cooking, not only because the end result is always delicious, but the preparation of the meal is fairly easy, allowing me to have fun along the way.

It was during the time I was cooking one of those easy and delicious recipes that I thought about the recipe of life. Our lives consist of different areas; relationships, work, finances, leisure, spiritual and so on. Now depending on the kind of ingredients we put into each of those areas, we can experience either something yummy or something that leaves a bad taste in our mouth.

When we throw in a tablespoon of control, a ½ a teaspoon of jealousy, a cup of anger and ½ a cup of fear into our relationships, we've created a recipe that makes it difficult to experience something wonderful that we'd like to have over and over again and share with our family and friends.

But, when we mix together love, patience, compassion and laughter, we end up with something that melts in our mouth leaving us feeling utterly satisfied and wanting seconds.

Like any great cook, you'll need to play around with your life's recipes to discover what ingredients work best together so you end up with the exact results you desire.

CHAPTER 3

EMOTIONAL ENERGY MANAGEMENT

TWO WOLVES —
A CHEROKEE TALE

One evening an old Cherokee told his grandson about a battle that goes on inside people. He said, "My son, the battle is between two 'wolves' inside us all.

"One is Evil. It is anger, envy, jealousy, sorrow, regret, greed, arrogance, self-pity, guilt, resentment, inferiority, lies, false pride, superiority, ego.

"The other is Good. It is joy, peace, love, hope, serenity, humility, kindness, benevolence, empathy, generosity, truth, compassion and faith."

The grandson thought about it for a minute and then asked his grandfather:

"Which wolf wins?"

The old Cherokee simply replied, "The one you feed."

Now I ask you; Which wolf are you feeding? Your Gremlin or your Genie?

STRIVING FOR PATIENCE

As I stood in the quick checkout line at the grocery store, it became anything but quick. The woman in front of me moved slower than molasses and seemed unaware of anyone else behind her.

I found myself looking around at the other checkout lines to see which one I might rush over to so I could get out of the store quicker. Just as I eyed an empty checkout and geared up for my getaway, a little voice inside said, "Stay." It was the softest voice and one I'm very familiar with. It was my Genie's voice and I always listen to my Genie because I know there's something wonderful to be gained from her.

So I stayed, and decided to step outside of myself to observe my actions and emotions while my Gremlin desperately wanted me to escape what I was experiencing. The checkout woman had a pleasant smile on her face and kept looking at me as if to say, "I'm so sorry this is happening."

"Me too!" my Gremlin wanted to scream. But I wouldn't allow that.

Instead, I chose to breathe deeply and send as much love and light as I could to this slow moving woman. In doing so, I began to feel more calm and unattached to what was happening. Eventually I completely accepted the situation and no longer cared how long it would take.

When she finished, she turned and said to me, "Thank you for being so patient with me. I know I can be quite slow at times."

(So much for her not being aware!) My heart just melted. I smiled and told her it was no problem and off she went. What I really wanted to say was:

"Thank *you*, for giving me the gift to remind myself that no matter what's happening outside of me, it's always my choice to change how I'm feeling, thinking and reacting when it's not in my best interest."

LETTING GO OF SAMENESS

There was a period when one of my clients was going through a very difficult time.

Experiencing feelings of fear, confusion and pain, she expressed that she wished everything prior to this situation could have stayed the same so she wasn't so sad.

I felt so much compassion for her when she said that because I understood her primal need for sameness in that moment, especially when everything seemed to be going so well just days before. But as life will have it from time to time, things happen that can throw us for a loop, struggling to make sense of it all.

During our conversation I felt compelled to say something to her. And even though I wasn't sure her emotional state would allow her to take it in, I went for it anyway. Perhaps what I said to her might be words you can consider for yourself during difficult times.

"When we, and circumstances in our life, stay the same day in and day out, we deny ourselves the opportunity to grow and improve, and to receive something even greater."

We never know what life will bring us each and every day. But it's in those painful moments, when we can muster up enough courage to see beyond the pain, that we open ourselves up to the gift that's there for us to receive.

As for my client, she *did* take in my words, and was able to experience a glimmer of light.

Releasing Past Hurts

Two Zen monks were walking through a forest when they came upon a woman standing on the bank of a stream that she was unable to cross. After considering her dilemma, one monk picked her up in his arms, carried her across the stream, and placed her gently on the ground. The other monk watched in horror, because the rules of their order forbade touching women.

The two monks continued on their way, but the second monk was furious for a long time. Finally he said, "You know that touching a woman is against our principles!" With that, the other monk turned to him and gently said, "I put her down an hour ago. You, however, are still carrying her."

~ Author Unknown

As long as you continue to carry past hurts and anger into the present, you will walk through life with a heavy, emotional load, missing opportunities that can bring you a life full of joy and ease.

HEALING, IT'S A PROCESS

At one time in my life I was given the gift of experiencing tendonitis of the knee. Now before I continue, I should let you know that when this first showed up I was less than thrilled and in no way felt it was a gift. The fact is, it cut into my walking and swimming a great deal and that just wasn't okay with me. However, I came to realize that my unwillingness to stop exercising caught up with me and made this whole knee issue worse. Yes, I can be as stubborn as the next person.

It wasn't until my physical therapist uttered the words, "Linda, you've got to stop exercising for a while. This is a process and it takes time to allow for the healing so you can be back at full capacity. And the fact is, if you give yourself the chance to heal and do the therapy without exercising or trying to rush the process, you'll be stronger than before the injury."

Who the heck did this guy think he was, my life coach or something! Actually, that's exactly who he became in my eyes at that moment. His words had a profound affect on me and I instantly understood, that no matter what the injury, physical, emotional or spiritual, rushing the process is never going to get any of us to full capacity and be stronger than before.

Healing takes time and the bottom line is it takes as long as it takes. And what I know for sure, is the sooner we embrace the process and do everything we can to assist the healing according to the Genie within and not the Gremlin, we'll be much better off.

PEACE DURING ADVERSITY

Wanting to feel at peace in life is perhaps one of the greatest desires people share with me. The tricky part is this: Being at peace even during times of adversity.

Life is never going to be adversity free. There will be circumstances that are going to challenge you from time to time. Some will be small and others will be whoppers. Peace, like happiness, is an internal choice. Peace is not something you find outside of yourself. Peace is not something that is determined by what you are faced with from day to day.

You must choose peace. And that choice must be made every single day you wake up. One of my mantras to help me with this is:

Today I will allow myself to maintain my inner peace in spite of what is showing up around me.

This doesn't mean you can't get angry or feel sadness. It doesn't mean that you walk around with a smile on your face 24/7. It simply means that even with those emotions, you stand in a place of understanding that things are happening as they need to. You recognize that you have the power to make choices along the way to either change the circumstance or wait patiently until you find a way that takes care of the issue. And, in that state of peace during adversity, is the understanding that sometimes doing nothing is the best solution, because many issues can clear up on their own.

I know this is not an easy concept. There are times when I, too, find myself struggling to remain in peace during adversity. And, what I have learned is, the more inner peace I feel, the quicker the adversity falls away.

I'M ONLY ONE PERSON

The post office was an absolute zoo as it can often be on a Saturday. I had to pick up a package and even the "pick up only" area was unusually crowded. I stood patiently waiting my turn, observing the woman behind the counter as she did her best to manage her energy in a flurry of demands from co-workers and customers.

Finally, calmly, but firmly, she said to everyone, "I'm only one person, so please be patient." The chaos seemed to simmer down a bit. Her co-workers backed off and the customers were more understanding. I kept my focus on her and sent her tons of appreciation and love for the great job she was doing.

When it was my turn, she looked at me and smiled as though I was the only person in the room with her. Her intention to be of service to others on her terms was very powerful. Even though people were pulling at her from every direction, she was completely present, working with one person at a time without getting caught up in trying to please as many people as possible all at the same time, just so *they* felt like things were moving more quickly.

With her smile and composed demeanor, she easily calmed others during their impatient moments. I was witnessing someone who was a perfect example of emotional energy management. There's no question in my mind, because this woman was in complete control of her energy, every person she helped was out of that post office more quickly than if she got caught up in the energy of the masses.

When you find yourself being pulled in twenty different directions, sometimes you have to remind people, calmly, "I'm only one person." Your emotional intent alone can reveal that you, too, want to complete the tasks at hand with ease, order, and as quickly as possible.

USING YOUR TIME

I was sitting in a parking lot one day becoming rather frustrated — because this parking lot was actually the Los Angeles freeway. I could feel myself becoming irritated, looking around at which lane would get me where I wanted to go, faster. As I switched lanes a few times, I realized that no matter what lane I was in it always seemed as though the one I just escaped was now moving faster.

I laughed at myself and recognized how I was creating the stress that was building internally. And then I realized I had a choice. Keep playing the "find the fastest lane" game or sit back, relax and appreciate that I have time to myself with no interruptions. I liked the latter choice much better.

So as I sat in my car, crawling along the freeway, I focused on my breathing. Then I thought about some wonderful, recent experiences, and other things I was looking forward to. Before I knew it, I was smiling and the stress had disappeared. I became grateful for the traffic because it gave me the ability to reflect and notice how wonderful life had been lately. This was a gift.

We are often so busy going from one place to another or planning whatever we need to plan for, that it's easy to lose those opportunities we're given by the universe to relax, reflect and appreciate.

Traffic, long lines, or waiting for someone who's late all give you the ability to practice patience and stay present. I know there are times when you're in a hurry, but the truth is, the lines and traffic don't go away just because of your hurry. So why not breathe deeply and use your time to do your best to allow and let go.

The End Result

I have to admit; there are times when I'm more focused on the end result of a project I'm working on than on the actual process and journey. When I do this, I notice I'm more anxious, uptight, concerned, and lacking in trust that everything will work out just as it needs to.

The minute I bring myself back into the present moment, and take whatever next step that inspires me, I have more fun and remember that's what matters most.

Be willing to observe yourself as you work on projects that you'd like to experience more ease with but find yourself struggling. How much time do you spend worrying about the end result that keeps you from moving forward, not allowing you to make clear decisions or take inspired actions?

Whatever fears creep in about the end result is your Gremlin doing a number on you yet again, thinking it's protecting you from being disappointed. Do your best to just look at what sits in front of you in the here and now and take whatever action feels best. There's no law that says you can't change your mind along the way when you discover a new option that would better serve you and the project.

NOT SUPPOSED TO KNOW

I know there are some things you don't want to be experiencing in your life. I know that most people would like advanced information to be able to make decisions more easily. And you know what else I know? I know you're not supposed to know all that advanced information that may seem like it will help you make decisions more easily.

So how do I know all this? I don't really. I just know that one time when I came through the other side of something painful, frustrating and confusing, I backtracked and saw how I got to where I finally felt the joy and peace. By doing this I realized the perfection in *not* knowing what was coming down the pipe because there's a good chance I would have resisted every step of the way.

Why? Because it's not the way my small self would have liked to see things unfolding. And, the way things *did* unfold, I now know, was the best way to allow for my greatest growth and deeper understanding in the long run.

It really is okay to walk the path of not knowing. Every step you take along that path eventually brings you into knowing and when you reach that place of knowing, you have, in your back pocket, more confidence and trust in your ability to move through the next phase of not knowing in your life.

Oh, and here's one more thought to ponder. Just because you think you know something about how the events are being played out, doesn't necessarily mean it's true.

REGARDLESS

Regardless of what happened during your child-hood, you can choose to live from the now.

Regardless of what someone said about you that hurt, you get to let go and move on.

Regardless of any mistakes you made prior to this moment, you can start fresh.

Regardless of painful, past relationships, you're capable of loving and being loved again.

Regardless of how long you've been asleep, you can wake up now.

Regardless of how long you've been unhappy, you can choose happiness now.

Regardless of how many tears you've shed, you can choose to laugh more often.

Regardless of the fears you have, you can walk toward courage.

Regardless of how many times you fall down, you can keep picking yourself right back up.

Regardless of who tells you it can't be done, you can still choose to get it done.

Regardless of who doesn't believe in you, you can still believe in yourself.

Regardless of what you don't know, you can always learn.

Regardless of who you're angry with, you can always choose to forgive.

Regardless of who doesn't like or love you, you can always love yourself.

Regardless of anything in your life that isn't serving you, you can always choose differently.

Emotional Reminder for the Holidays

For the holiday season, I want to remind you about something my coaching clients often tell me is especially tough during the holiday time: Managing your emotional energy.

Whoever you're with and whatever obligations you feel you must follow through with, it's completely up to you to consciously manage your emotional energy so you allow yourself to have the best time possible with family and friends. And keep in mind, managing your emotional energy actually starts *before* you're with the people you'll be spending your time with.

Pay attention to what you think and say as you anticipate upcoming festivities. If you find yourself complaining about certain people, you're setting yourself up for the same old experience. Start feeling and seeing an experience that you would like to have.

No matter what people are saying or doing, you're always free to choose how you want to feel and respond. You can either get caught up in someone else's energy or you can stay true to yourself and let go of anything that isn't in your best interest.

My neighbor, (let's call her Pam), has Christmas at her house every year and each year she ends up angry. Her sister always finds something to criticize about the gathering and makes sure Pam knows about it. Without fail, Pam allows herself to be pulled into this criticism and ends up arguing with her sister.

As Christmas was getting closer, Pam was sharing her concern with me about her sister and how she no longer wanted to fall prey to her criticism. I shared the concept of emotional energy management with her and suggested she visualize herself having a joyful time in spite of her sister. Liking this idea, she decided to do the visualization and consequently, to do her best to manage her energy and make it the best Christmas ever.

I realize this isn't the easiest thing to do when you're in the throes of what's taking place in the moment, but that doesn't mean it's not possible. Don't engage until you're ready to do so in a way that feels more aligned with your heart and soul. Don't react from the pushed buttons.

Pause, take a deep breath, and ask yourself, "Who do I choose to be right now that would serve the highest good of all concerned?" It only takes a second to do this and it allows you the space to make a new choice and not react out of habit. It allows you to quiet your Gremlin. It allows you to change your story. It allows you to create a different relationship. It allows you to reconnect with your soul. And it allows you to have a whole new experience.

I spoke to Pam the day after her Christmas gathering, and she told me that it was indeed a joyful Christmas experience! She didn't engage in her sister's negativity and smiled her way through the day focusing on all the other wonderful people who were there, too. The best part of all? Her sister stopped looking for things to criticize.

I wish you many beautiful holidays this year.

Urrrrgh...Breaking Habits

Breaking a six-year habit wasn't as easy as I thought it would be. Now understand I didn't need to break this particular habit because I wanted to change myself in some monumental way. Ohhhh nooooo. This habit was so silly, that I'm almost embarrassed how long it took to break it — four weeks! Although that doesn't sound like a long time to break a habit of six years, when I tell you what it was, you might think otherwise.

Maybe you're wondering why I'm sharing this with you — or maybe you're not. But either way I'll tell you. The idea that it took me four weeks to break a habit as silly as this one got me thinking how ingrained habits really are. And, how important it is to be easy on yourself while you're in the process of changing an emotional, physical or financial habit that no longer serves you.

I encourage you to live by the creed to be loving and gentle with yourself. Watch out for your Gremlin's comments when you don't do something that supports your intent to break your habit. I have to admit, I was shocked, and then finally amused, at the length of time it took me to break my habit.

Yes, I'll reveal it, but only if you promise not to make too much fun of me. A little is okay, but let's not go overboard here. After all, we *are* working on our spiritual growth, which includes compassion and letting go of judgment, right? Okay, here it is:

I bought a new toothbrush head for my Sonicare electric toothbrush. The old one had a cap to cover the bristles and I accidentally threw out the old *and* new cap. Every single time I picked up the toothbrush I made the motion of removing the cap that wasn't there. And, what's worse, after I brushed my teeth, I would look for the cap to put back on that *still* wasn't there! I told you it was a silly habit.

So what's the lesson here? Please be loving and gentle with yourself when breaking habits that can change your life. Especially with the ones you've had for a lifetime.

Raising Your Energy
to Help Others

I was working with a client who was struggling with allowing abundance into her life on all levels. When good starts manifesting, her Gremlin makes an appearance telling her about all the people in the world, including those close to her, who are worse off than she is, and that she shouldn't be so quick to jump on the bandwagon of bliss.

This comes up a lot for people when I work with them on manifesting what they want in their life. So, I'd like to say something on this issue in case you find *your* Gremlin pulling the same tricks on you.

There will always be people who are having their own experiences around the lack of abundance that you can't do anything about. And, it's not necessarily up to you to *have* to do anything about it. Every person is going through what they're going through for one reason or another and there's always something to be learned and gained in every experience. No matter how painful it may appear.

So when you have a strong desire for joy, peace and abundance in your life, and you're focusing on someone else's lack of it, you're not only stopping the flow of all that you deserve in *your* life, it absolutely doesn't do anything to shift anyone else's life.

You are a vibrational Being! And when you start to raise your vibration to bring you more of what you *do* want, you actually stand a better chance of helping others just by the essence of your vibration. You *can* reach them on levels way beyond words. Hold your vision of prosperity and peace for all, and allow them the choice to move into that vibration when they're ready.

In the meantime, drive toward *your* heart's desire and tell your Gremlin to get in the back seat!

SHIFTING GEARS

About a year after I started driving, my dad bought me an old Volkswagen Bug, stick shift. Now, if you had to learn to drive a stick shift, too, you'll probably remember it was very tricky learning to shift gears without stalling out. I was the queen of stalls. But after about an hour I got the hang of it. Feeling rather smug and proud, my dad directed me toward a hill near our house called Tank Hill because of its steepness.

So much for being smug. I must have stalled out a thousand and one times on that hill and as the stalls increased so did my emotions. I cried. I cursed the hill, my dad, the car, and my inability to shift gears until my dad said something really powerful to me.

He told me that I needed to calm down and work on shifting the internal gears before I could succeed with the external. So in that moment, I *did* choose to calm down and shift my internal gears that had been the real driver of the car up to that point. Much to my amazement, with the internal shift, the external gears shifted smoothly over and over again, without a single stall. Now I was receiving the same quality performance from my car while on the hill, that I experienced on the flat roads. What fun I had!

Sometimes, life isn't much different than a stick shift — full of different gears to maneuver through to get the best performance possible out of life for yourself. It's important to allow yourself to shift your internal gears when the time arrives. If you insist on staying in first or second gear when it's time to move into third or forth gear because you're afraid, or because the old gear is familiar, then you're going to find yourself stalling out over and over again. It's easy to want to turn off the engine and throw away the key when you're stalled, but don't. Keep shifting gears until you find yourself smoothly moving forward again.

CHAPTER 4

RELATIONSHIPS

Forgiveness

When you won't forgive someone, you are living with that circumstance day in and day out; whether you're consciously aware of it or not. This can color your interactions with other relationships, especially when a situation pops up that you believe is similar to the past circumstance you won't forgive. But remember, the past doesn't equal the present.

It's only the story your Gremlin tells you that turns two different circumstances into the same.

As you hold onto the inability to forgive, over time, your heart will contract instead of expand, eventually leading to total shut down. Although the concept of forgiveness is simple, it's not always easy. It's important to be loving and gentle with yourself as you move into a state of forgiveness, and above all, forgive yourself for not moving as fast as you might like to with the process.

Forgiveness:

1. Is about you, not the other person.

2. Allows you to release any energy you're holding that doesn't serve you and keeps you from moving forward.

3. Gives you the opportunity to be grateful for the lessons gained from the experience and use those lessons for your greatest growth.

4. Allows you to choose to keep the person in your life or let the person go with a clear conscience. And yes, you can forgive and still move on from that relationship.

5. Gives you the freedom to set some new ground rules so the situation doesn't repeat itself.

6. Is telling yourself you deserve better.

7. And forgiveness means no longer using someone else's actions and behavior toward you as a reason for not living the life you desire and being the person you want to be.

Forgiveness means relinquishment. It's that simple. To relinquish something is to release whatever power it holds over us. If I forgive someone for a wrong done to me, I no longer allow that event to determine how I treat the other person. I may remember the wrong or I may forget it, but either way I have disarmed it. It no longer determines my actions, thought, or words.

~ MARK W. MEUSSE

THE COURAGE TO SAY NO

A common theme throughout my coaching practice is the difficulty people have saying the word no. For such a tiny word it carries a huge burden. All too often their mouth says yes while their heart says no.

Most of these people don't want to hurt or disappoint someone so they end up putting their own feelings aside just to keep the peace. Unfortunately, while the peace is being kept externally, there's a war slowly brewing internally. The internal war will eventually take a person down by manifesting their struggle in physical and/or emotional ways.

Since I used to be one of the biggest yes people I know, I've come to learn two things as a result of saying no due to following my heart; I am able to express myself clearly and confidently, and, others understand and respect my decision. There is very little attempt, if any, on their part, to change my mind and I believe that's because of the energy I hold with my no.

Saying yes, when you mean no, can lead to resentment and result in doing something half-hearted. That's a disservice to all parties involved. Think of your no as giving the other person an opportunity to receive what they need from someone else who will put their whole heart and soul into it. And, sometimes your no is a gift, allowing the other person to realize they're very capable of doing on their own, what they asked of you.

If you have a hard time saying no because you're concerned people won't like you, here's a few questions for you. I encourage you to answer them honestly.

1. Do you really want people in your life who wouldn't like you just because you said no to them?

2. Do you truly believe having people like that in your life is bringing you more joy?

3. Do you believe you deserve people in your life who allow you the freedom to make your own decisions and still love and support you along the way?

Taking a wild guess here, I believe these are your answers: No. No. Yes. Why do I believe this? Because I've never met anyone who doesn't want a life that can bring them as much happiness as possible.

When you speak your truth and stay in integrity, you attract the same kind of people to you and all others begin to fall away. As you find the courage to say no, your life will improve one hundred-fold. True friends will stay. You won't lose anyone in your life that you'll regret losing and you've made room for new true friends to come through the door.

As Author Alan Cohen stated quite beautifully:

It's far better to have a few good friends who accept you for who you are than a lot of friends who accept you because you are doing the dance they expect.

CREATING OUR OWN
DISAPPOINTMENT

Ꮋ ow many times have you found yourself disappointed with someone in your life? Disappointed because someone said she would do something for you and she didn't. Disappointed because someone said he'd be there for you and that didn't happen. Disappointed because you believed someone would actually do for herself what was promised and nothing was done.

Perhaps you've experienced disappointment in others more times than you care to think about. Well, I'm about to challenge you on the reality of disappointments. What if I said, the disappointment has nothing to do with the other person and everything to do with you? Maybe you're ready to send me a nasty email or maybe you're intrigued.

The truth is, people can only do what they can do. And even when their intention is to follow through with what they say, they still only do what they do. They either do what they say or they don't. It's really that simple.

Therefore, it's up to us, after just one time of being disappointed by someone, to consider that her word may not be as reliable as we had hoped. And, that she's really not willing to behave any differently for the time being.

People will often reveal their behaviors and patterns very quickly, and it's us who aren't always willing to see what is being revealed right from the start. As we continue to put our faith and trust in someone who is not holding his own, then the real disappointment rests on our shoulders. When we keep expecting someone to do something different than what he is doing, we disappoint ourselves. Not the other person. It's never about the other person. He hasn't done anything we weren't already aware of, we just keep pretending like we don't already know or conveniently keep forgetting.

PERFECT ANGER

Sounds a little odd, doesn't it? Perfect anger. I would have thought so, too, until I came across a quote by Aristotle:

> *Anyone can become angry — that's easy. But to be angry with the right person, to the right degree, at the right time, for the right purpose, and in the right way — that is not easy.*

How often do we find ourselves angry about a situation or at a person that doesn't truly deserve our anger? Probably more times than any of us would care to admit. And since I started this conversation I'll fess up to something that happened with me.

My son caught me red handed with my less than perfect anger. As a matter of fact, he didn't even belong on my anger scale! I was upset with my husband and did what any loving parent would do — I took it out on my poor son who walked in the door fifteen minutes after my little spat with his dad. It certainly seemed reasonable to me at the time. After all, don't most teenagers give their parents lots of reasons to be upset with them?

Well, if the truth be told, I have very little reason to be upset with my son the majority of the time, so it was really easy for him to hit me right between the eyes with these words:

"Mom, don't take out your anger on me just because you and dad had a stupid fight."

Wow! Talk about hitting the nail on the head. And the best part was hearing the words stupid fight. The fact is, the fight *was* stupid, and didn't deserve the kind of anger I was feeling. So in that moment, I remembered Aristotle's words and thought to myself:

"I took my anger out on the wrong person and the degree of my anger with my husband was also wrong. Apologies all the way around!"

Place Aristotle's quote somewhere in your home, and the next time you find yourself getting angry over something, read it and see if you need to shift into a place of perfect anger. I promise you this, perfect anger will have you moving through conflicts quicker than you can say, "I'm sorry!"

HEART LISTENING

Think about the last, in-depth conversation you had with someone. Can you remember how present you were when the other person was speaking? Were you thinking about what you wanted to say next while she was speaking?

Sometimes we'll ask for people's advice with the intention of receiving some great input only to end up either defending our situation or interrupting and dismissing the suggestions or insights being shared. This happens when we let our own judgments or biases cloud our ability to be fully present and open.

And, when you're not fully present, you rob yourself of the opportunity to learn something new, and often, very valuable. So here's the deal — the next time you're speaking with your spouse, child, partner, friend, co-worker or boss, make an extra effort to silence that little Gremlin in your head and listen from your heart. The experience is quite profound and brings communication to a whole new level.

An Act of Kindness

I witnessed something that absolutely made my heart sing and lifted my day. A much older lady, I'm guessing somewhere in her eighties, was struggling to put her grocery bags in the trunk of her car.

As I walked toward her to help, a gentleman, who at first glance, you wouldn't connect with the word gentleman, got to her before me. He had just stepped off his Harley, was very gruff and tough looking, and someone who I might consider avoiding if I were walking alone on the street.

After I was done judging this man, I was struck by the way he approached her before helping. He gently touched her shoulder, introduced himself, and said he would like to put the bags in the trunk for her if she didn't mind.

Now here's the best part. She not only gave him a sweet and loving smile, she told him what a dear he was to offer his help and she would be thrilled to have such a 'strong, handsome man' help her out. Then he smiled the biggest smile, suddenly looking like a schoolboy with a crush and put the bags in the trunk.

When he was done she put her arms out toward him and he took the cue. They embraced for a few seconds and then she kissed him on the cheek only to finish it off by saying, "If there's a lady in your life she's a very lucky gal!"

Honestly, just the memory of it makes me all mushy inside. It was so clear to me, in that moment, what an honor it was to witness this. And to be reminded that no matter what we look like on the outside, there is a place inside all of us where a tremendous amount of love and kindness resides. Some people are just able to express it more freely than others. I believe this love and kindness is in every human being on the planet and I intend to do my best to live with that belief and treat people accordingly.

How about you?

A Lie Hits Deep

Walking into Radio Shack I noticed a woman sitting in her car with her legs outside the door. I thought she was having trouble getting out so I asked if she needed some help. She didn't and was just waiting for the store to open. Together we walked toward the store. She told me that she was there to replace the telephone wire that she's sure one of her grandchildren had cut. They were four and five years old.

There was such sadness in her voice that I asked her, "Is it just the cut wire that's bothering you or something else?" She said, "Oh, yes. It is something else. Neither of the boys would admit they did this and it just breaks my heart to think they would lie to me." She went on to say, "I am not naïve, and nothing hurts me more than when people lie. I've felt this way my whole life and every time I'm lied to it just breaks my heart."

Then she looked at me at asked, "Have you ever lied?" How I didn't want to disappoint her! How I wanted to say, "No, never!" But that would have been a lie.

"I'm afraid I have lied in my life." I replied. Quickly following up with, "But I now know the importance of truth and do my best to always speak it." She smiled, touched my arm and said, "That's good."

When we got inside the store she showed the manager the wire and he said, "Looks like someone took a scissors to this and cut it." She nodded her head slowly and now my heart was breaking. I saw in her eyes how much pain she felt from the lie she was told and it instilled in me even deeper, how important it is to be truthful, especially with the ones we love the most. No matter how much we believe we're protecting someone, the possibilities are too great that down the line someone will end up hurt.

As Don Miguel Ruiz says in his book, *The Four Agreements,* "Be impeccable with your word."

DEALING WITH CRISIS

A friend of mine lost his son to cancer. Needless to say it's been an incredibly difficult journey for him and his family. When we spoke he shared with me that not only has this experience been overwhelmingly challenging, but he's also been burdened with thoughts of certain people he believed he could count on who haven't been there for him.

When it comes to a crisis, especially one involving an untimely death, it's not unusual for people to be very uncomfortable and not know what to say or do. Although you may wish people would put their own "stuff" aside during your difficult time and support you, it isn't always the case. Those who are closest to you, and hurting because of the pain you are experiencing, can often have the hardest time knowing what to do or say.

Those less close to you, can often step up and support you in ways you never imagined possible. Being less emotionally involved can make it easier to be there for someone in pain.

So I ask that you remember, should you find yourself experiencing your own personal tragedy, to not hold onto too much expectation with certain people in your life. Don't hold a grudge, it only adds to the pain you're already living with. Trust they will come around with the passing of time and perhaps then, you can talk about it more easily.

There are many reasons why people pull back during times of tragedy. And what I've come to learn above all else is, it's not because they *don't* care, it's because they care so much, that they're afraid of causing you more pain by doing or saying the wrong thing.

It's Just Nice to Connect

A gentleman gave me a great big wave and smile as he drove up to the stop sign where I was walking. I didn't wave back because I was too busy trying to figure out where I knew him from since he seemed to know me.

"No, we don't know each other." he said. "I just like to wave to people and send a friendly hello any chance I get. It's just nice to connect." I laughed and said, "I love that! Thank you, you've made my day!" We both continued on our way but not before I gave a wave and big smile right back at him!

"It's just nice to connect." What a lovely thing to say. Especially coming from a complete stranger. It truly lifted my spirits throughout the rest of the day!

Making an effort to connect with others when we don't know them is something we need to do more of in the world. And when we can do it with the enthusiasm that this gentleman did with me, it can turn someone's yucky day into a better day and someone's good day into a glorious day!

See how many people you can connect with this week and notice how it makes *you* feel.

No Need to Yell

While speaking to a friend at a social gathering, we witnessed a couple that we both knew, having a rather heated discussion. It got to a point where they had to leave. My friend said something to me that melted my heart.

He said, "I don't ever remember yelling at my wife like that or even needing to raise my voice to her."

"Really!" I said. "That's pretty remarkable coming from a guy who's been married twenty-eight years."

His reply?

"Well, the way I see it, Jackie loves me more than any other person on the planet. And it's never her intention to purposely hurt me. So in the moment of things not being at their best, I remind myself of that and it allows me to stay as calm as I can. And, I know how much it would hurt her for me to yell at her for something she didn't do with malice."

His explanation stopped me dead in my tracks and completely reframed my thinking when it comes to being in disagreement with someone I love or feel hurt by. It made so much sense and gave me a new understanding that there really can be no need to yell.

I invite you to take what my friend said to heart, and see how you might be able to change your perspective with your loved ones during those moments of less than blissful times.

UNCONDITIONAL LOVE

As I waited for my turn to see the eye doctor, a little boy, about 8 years old, was sitting across from me while his mother was in with the doctor. From the corner of my eye I saw him pick up his mom's cell phone and call someone.

I thought to myself, "Who could this child be calling?" Within seconds the answer revealed itself. "Hi, Daddy! I was just thinking about you and wanted to say I love you. I miss you. When are you coming home from your trip?" "Okay. Well I love you forever and will hug you when you get home. Bye-bye."

Being witness to that was almost more than I could stand. My heart was exploding with love and admiration for this little guy as my eyes were filling up quickly. The pureness and simplicity of expressing his love was just beautiful. Children are our greatest teachers in unconditional love. There is no hidden agenda. No over thinking what to say, when to say it, where to say it or how to say it. It's love at its finest. And when the feeling of love came over him, he just followed his heart. Nothing more and nothing less.

TRUSTING THE HAND YOU HOLD

Although this story is short, it's beautiful and quite profound.

> *A little girl and her father were crossing a bridge. The father was kind of scared so he asked his little daughter: "Sweetheart, please hold my hand so that you don't fall into the river."*
>
> *The little girl said: "No, Dad. You hold my hand."*
>
> *"What's the difference?" asked the puzzled father.*
>
> *"There's a big difference," replied the little girl. "If I hold your hand and something happens to me, chances are that I may let your hand go. But if you hold my hand, I know for sure that no matter what happens, you will never let my hand go."*
>
> ~ AUTHOR UNKNOWN

Be the hand that someone can hold to feel the trust and love through. And allow into your life, a hand that can do the same for you when needed.

CREATING BOUNDARIES

If you're often the go-to person when others are in need of emotional support, it's really important to keep your boundaries in place. There's nothing wrong with lending a sympathetic ear and even offering up some sound advice, but make sure you're not being drained in the process. People love the opportunity to dump their stuff onto a kind-hearted soul.

I call them energy vampires. They'll suck the life out of you when you let them, without giving any thought to your well-being. They're usually more interested in hearing themselves talk and having someone to complain to without any intention of changing their situation.

If you've got anyone in your life that fits this bill, it's your responsibility to have your boundaries in place and not allow the life to be drained out of you. Here's a few ways to set up your boundaries:

1. Tell him you're no longer available to complain to until you see him making an effort to change his circumstances.

2. Listen without offering any advice or kind words for a limited amount of time. When she's done talking, let her know you trust that she's more than capable of working the problem out if she really wants to. Then tell her you've got some personal things you must take care of and politely leave or hang up the phone.

3. Let him know you're working on your own personal issues and aren't much good to anyone else at the moment. (Working on creating boundaries *is* your personal issue.)

It takes courage to be different with people when they're used to you being a certain way. People don't change unless they want to. Therefore, it's up to you to change yourself so you attract people and circumstances that are aligned with your heart and soul.

If creating boundaries is very difficult for you, ask yourself:

1. What is the payoff for me by being the go-to person all the time? (There *is* a payoff when you look at it honestly.)

2. What am I afraid of if I create boundaries?

Are You Really Helping?

During my walk I started to pick up someone's newspaper in her driveway to move it closer to her front door. Why? Well, the last time I walked past this person's driveway she seemed to be struggling to get to the paper. You see, she was quite old and it appeared that every step she took was difficult. On that day I *did* pick up the paper and handed it to her when she got to it. She smiled sweetly and thanked me.

As I came to her driveway on this particular day, I saw the paper and started to move it so she wouldn't have to walk so far. Suddenly, a little voice inside said, "Are you really helping?"

Immediately it occurred to me that I might actually be doing her a disservice. What if that walk to the end of her driveway is good for her? What if that's her way of guaranteeing she would get some movement in her body? What if she felt like she accomplished something for herself just by being able to get to the newspaper?

I decided to leave the paper where it was.

Do you ever find yourself doing things for people when they haven't asked for your help? How often do you feel the need to jump in and help someone if it appears he's struggling with something?

Who says struggle is a bad thing? Life is full of them and getting beyond the struggle can bring a great sense of accomplishment, giving us more confidence when the next struggle shows up. And, what you may define as a struggle isn't necessarily what someone else defines as a struggle.

So the next time you're ready to go full out to help someone, pause for a minute and ask, "Am I really helping?" You may be surprised what answer you discover below the surface.

RELATIONSHIPS AS AN AWAKENING

~~~

If there's anything in the world that gives us the greatest opportunity to see who we really are and what our greatest fears and judgments are, it's being in relationship.

Relationship with your boss, co-worker, business partner, friend, lover, family members, telemarketer, salesperson, teachers, doctors and even strangers. All of these people can be in relationship with you whether it's for minutes, hours, days, weeks, months, years.

When there's a dialogue taking place, there's a relationship happening in the moment. And, in each of those moments, you have an opportunity to learn more about yourself than you may realize. As you take in what others are doing or saying and observe how you react or respond to it, verbally and silently, there's a golden opportunity for you to experience all those relationships as an awakening for your greater growth.

Just for fun, take an entire day and observe yourself with every person you spend time in relationship with. You might be surprised what you learn about yourself!

GET IN LINE!

At the grocery store I witnessed a dynamic between a husband and wife that broke my heart. The checkout lines were longer than usual and as the husband, wife, and I approached the same line, the wife told her husband, in a demanding voice, "Get in line while I go get one more thing."

With all the noise, he didn't hear her and the conversation went like this:

H — "What?"

W — "I said, GET IN LINE! And hold the hand basket while I get one more thing."

H — (In a very mocking voice) "Well, aren't we touchy! Would it kill you to add a please with that demand?"

She then proceeded to give him a very nasty look, which prompted him to do the same to her. Now I obviously have no idea what the deal is between the two of them, but it sure made me stop and think how I treat the people closest to me in my life. I'd like to believe that I'm patient and loving the majority of the time. And although that may be true, I know there are times when I can be more patient with a stranger than the people I love the most.

I do know that I've never gone to the extreme that the couple in the grocery store demonstrated, but it's certainly worth a pause to consider how we treat our loved ones most of the time. It's too easy to take people for granted when they're in our life day in and day out. And, if we don't want our family and friends to take *us* for granted, then we need to behave toward others how we wish them to behave toward us.

If you've been less than loving with your loved ones, this might be a good time to give them a hug and let them know how much you appreciate them. You and I both know it'll make them feel good. And the other advantage is how good it's going to make *you* feel!

LOVE IS THE STUFF INSIDE

$tanding in line to go through airport security, there was a man in front of me carrying a colorful box with a handle. What grabbed my attention was what it said on the outside of the box; Love is the stuff inside.

I felt so good when I read those words because I believe there is no greater truth. Love *is* the stuff inside!

When we get down to the core of what's real in life, it's love, and that love can come from only one place: Inside of each and every one of us. Some people have an easier time than others allowing that love to come through, but the bottom line, it's still inside there. No matter how deep you have to dig, it's there. And it's up to all of us to be willing to keep going within to feel the love we carry.

If you've been a little stingy with your love lately, now is always a good time to reach inside, pull it out, and share it with as many people as you possibly can!

EXCUSES, EXCUSES, EXCUSES

How do you feel when someone keeps giving you excuses as to why something didn't get done per your request or why it's taking longer than they said it would? How do you feel when someone keeps showing up late to a meeting with you and gives you a million excuses each time it happens? How do you feel when you want to see someone and they keep giving you excuse after excuse why they can't?

Frustrated? Hurt? Angry? Taken advantage of?

All of the above?

Now let's take the other person out of the equation and ask yourself this: How often do you make up excuses to yourself about your own life? The excuses you tell yourself as you try to make significant changes in your life and just don't seem to pull it off. The excuses you tell yourself as to why you can't start that project you've been promising yourself you'd eventually get to. The excuses you tell yourself about why you're having such a hard time turning your biggest dream into a reality.

Here's what Don Wilder has to say about excuses: "Excuses are the nails used to build the house of failure."

Don't treat yourself like you may allow others to treat you with *their* excuses. You deserve so much more than that. How about hammering in the nails that will build your house of accomplishments.

GIVING PRAISE

A girlfriend and I were having lunch and I asked about her son who was getting professional help for some behavioral problems. She shared with me that he seemed to be doing better and went on to say:

"There's a good change in his attitude."

"He's staying out of trouble, but I'm just waiting for the other shoe to drop."

"It's hard to trust him yet."

"He is doing things that he's never done before, which is great. But I still need to stay on top of him just in case."

As I listened, it occurred to me to ask a couple of questions.

"Have you told him how proud you are with how far he's come?"

"Have you thanked him for the things he's now doing that he didn't do in the past?"

She said no. And because she's a very bright woman she followed it up with:

"I really need to say those things."

"I *am* proud of him."

"I *am* grateful for what he's doing now."

"All I keep doing is looking at what he's still doing wrong and get on him about *that*."

"How's he ever going to feel good about himself and continue to improve if I don't encourage him for everything he's doing right!"

And then she went on to say:

"If I keep waiting for the other shoe to drop, it will!"

I just smiled and told her I loved her and that she's a great mom. The conversation moved on to a new topic.

It's worth taking a look at your close relationships and asking yourself:

Do I spend more time letting them know what they're doing wrong?

Or, do I express my appreciation when they go out of their way for me or do something simple, yet thoughtful?

People love to be acknowledged. It's the driving force that keeps them wanting to do well and do something nice for others.

You May Not Like Them, But Can You Love Them?

I'm sure there are many people whom you've come across in your life that you don't like. You don't like the way they act, the things they say, the way they treat you or someone else, the list can be endless. I get this. We all have people we don't gel with and who we'd rather not spend time with.

Now I have a question for you. Can you transcend yourself to a place that holds a greater understanding and love them even though you don't like them?

I know, I know, this is not the easiest concept to embrace and I struggled with this for a really long time. Oh, heck, I still struggle with it from time to time when I get all caught up with Gertrude, my Gremlin!

When you choose to transcend your mind, raising your consciousness above what you are observing in the moment from your Gremlin's perspective, there is no longer this feeling of separateness from another and need for judgment. There emerges an understanding that we are all Souls, made of love from one Source, having a human experience and doing the very best we know how, in the moment.

Ohhhh yes, this takes a strong commitment on your part to move into such a place. A place, that by the mere fact you've chosen a spiritual path for yourself, you would have been faced with sooner or later.

You see, there's just no sense in doing this journey part way. When you do, you cheat yourself out of the best experiences of your life. Learning to love others when you don't like them is embracing the journey all the way and stepping out of your comfort zone to transform your life.

I'll end with these two questions:

What if the person or people you don't like are actually there to awaken something in you for your higher good?

With that in mind, you may not like them, but can you love them for their Divinity and the opportunity they're presenting you?

~ CHAPTER 5 ~

CHANGING
YOUR STORY

YOUR GREMLIN'S STORY

Your Gremlin loves to control the details of the stories that come about through your life experiences. When something happens in life, like a breakup, loss of a job, missing a flight, being late to an appointment and any other gazillion things that can take place on a daily basis, your Gremlin will take any situation and turn it into a dramatic fiction novel when given the chance.

You see, stuff happens in life all the time. Some stuff is wonderful and some stuff is not so wonderful. It's the not so wonderful stuff that your Gremlin thrives on because it knows that's when you're most vulnerable. Then your Gremlin steps in and starts a whole scenario as to why this happened to you, what other problems this is going to bring you, who's at fault, and on and on it goes as you willingly and unconsciously play right into its manipulative little hands.

Your Gremlin loves drama and it's your job to stop the drama that's being created around the story. How do you do this? By quieting down your ongoing chatter and only looking at the facts without adding anything extra to the situation.

> **Fact:** You lost your job. Now you need to find a new job. End of story.
> **Gremlin's Drama:** I'll never find a job I like as much! I don't have any money! I'm broke! It's so hard to find a job in this market!

Fact: You missed your flight. You need to get the next available one. End of story.

Gremlin's Drama: There won't be another available flight! The person expecting me is going to have a cow! I'm such an idiot for not leaving earlier! Flying stinks!

Pay attention to when you allow your Gremlin to carry on and on about something that happened and ask yourself how much of what's being said is a fact or a dramatization.

Yes, it may be a fact that your financial circumstances are tight since the job loss, but continuing to build a story around that just creates more drama keeping you emotionally stuck. Focus on moving forward to find another job. All the talk about your lack of income is not going to improve the situation.

In any seemingly negative experience, you want to stop the dramatic stories as soon as possible and move in a direction that's going to serve you. And, I said seemingly negative experience, because we all know that those experiences can turn out to be our blessing in disguise!

THE PROBLEM WITH STORIES

Every one of us has a story or two to share about our lives. Some of these stories are funny or heartwarming and deserve to be told often because we feel good remembering them and it makes the listener feel good too.

Unfortunately, these aren't the kind of stories most people tend to focus on when sharing parts of their life with others. The stories that are given the most attention are full of drama, the poor me scenario, why does this keep happening in my life, and so on.

You know what I'm talking about. We all do it and we know darn well how we feel inside whether we're the one telling the story or the one listening. Not so great! So, if we know it doesn't feel so great then why keep telling the story?

Because it's comfortable and familiar. It's what we've been trained to do from a young age. Heck, the media continuously focuses on more bad feeling stories than good and people are glued to them. They talk about it at work, over drinks, dinner and parties.

But you know what? You have a choice to not do that anymore. Right here, right now, I'm going to challenge you to pay attention to the stories you share with others and see how often you're telling a story that constantly focuses on everything that's gone wrong in your life and what's not working; relationships, money, job and even the issues of the world.

When you let go of your stories from the past and stop bringing them into your present circumstances, a funny thing happens along the way. You become emotionally available to create a new story that supports what you want in your life instead of what you don't want.

Oh, and by the way, here's a suggestion to help you spend less time focusing on what's not working — turn off the news. If there's something you really need to know, it *will* find its way to you.

COLLAPSE THE STORIES

I was so deeply entrenched in my "story" that it paralyzed me from taking action for two days. I wanted to make a phone call to someone I didn't know. Someone I wanted to connect with on a business and personal level and I found myself creating all sorts of stories about the outcome that didn't exactly leave me feeling good. The deeper I got into my "story" the more my fear took over. It got to a point where I was picking up the phone to dial, only to find myself hanging up over and over again before I finished dialing.

On day two I finally remembered that everything I was telling myself had absolutely no truth to it! They were stories I completely manufactured about what would happen when I connected with the person I was afraid to call. Remembering this truth, I dialed the number feeling more peaceful.

The real story? I connected with someone who was a joy to talk to and an opportunity for an alliance was created that will serve both of us. Even though I've been doing spiritual growth work for more years than I care to admit sometimes, the fact is, I'm as human and vulnerable as any of you reading this. We can all find ourselves so caught up in our stories, that it's easy to *not* take the necessary actions that can bring us new opportunities and wonderful surprises for our soul's journey.

It's absolutely critical to collapse the stories you find yourself trapped in if you're going to make any real headway for yourself. All you need to remember is that any negatives you tell yourself before a situation has even unfolded, are lies. They are complete Gremlin fabrications.

If you end up with less than desired outcomes, don't worry about it! You did a great thing. You took action! Now you get to move on from that moment in time instead of staying in a state of anxiety from not taking action. And, what's really important to remember, when you fall short of your desired outcome, don't create another story about the outcome you just experienced. It's an outcome and nothing more.

Stick to the facts. You got a no. End of story. You didn't get the raise. End of story. They rejected your proposal. End of story. You didn't get the house. End of story. The list can go on and on. The sooner you end the story, the sooner you can move on to the wonder and delight that awaits you for your higher good.

YEAH, BUT...

Yeah, but... We've all heard these words come out of others' mouths while talking with them. And, it's certainly come out of our own mouth on numerous occasions.

As I spoke with a friend I found myself immersed in her "Yeah, but." She's been thinking about selling her business and working from home. It's a great move for her and although she knows this too, it seemed no matter what I said to support and encourage her dream, she had a "Yeah, but" for all of it.

You know what happened? I explained that her "Yeah, but" was starting to squelch my enthusiasm. She looked at me blankly and then said that she had no idea she was saying that. After thinking about what I said for a few seconds, she realized she did the "Yeah, but" scenario a lot when it came to big decisions in her life.

"Yeah, but" is a sure way of squelching any dream. "Yeah, but" interFEARS with magnificent possibilities. "Yeah, but" is limited thinking at its best. "Yeah, but" is the beginning of a story that will not serve you, and last, but not least, "Yeah, but" just happens to be one of your Gremlin's favorite two words.

Notice how often "Yeah, but" flies out of your mouth and each time you're aware of it, ask yourself what you're not letting in because of those two little words.

RAINY DAY SMILES

One year, during the Los Angeles Tournament of Roses Parade, it was pouring rain. Remarkably, before that particular parade day, it hadn't rained on the parade in fifty-one years!

I had never seen the parade while it was raining and I was curious to see if it would put an emotional damper on the event in any way. I wondered if there would still be a lot of people watching from the sidelines, and if the smiles were as big this year as they were every other year when the weather had been nice.

I turned on my TV and what I saw brought a smile to *my* whole Being. There was a huge crowd and everyone was having a wonderful time — parade participants and spectators. Their smiles were as big as I've ever seen them in the past and there seemed to be a little extra joy going on in spite of the rain.

These people were such perfect examples of not letting any negative outside element affect their joy. They decided a good time was there for the taking like prior years and that's exactly what they experienced.

It's a great lesson for all of us as we move through each and every day. Pay attention to how much you let the outside elements affect your behavior. Know it's always in your power to shift your emotions and tell yourself a story that allows you to feel even a little bit better. All you need to do is start small and before you know it, you'll find yourself smiling from ear to ear, letting go of any stories that don't serve you.

THE POWER OF YOUR MIND

I know how powerful the mind is and what I can accomplish when my mind and emotions are in alignment for my highest good. Even with that awareness, on this particular day, I had an epiphany that strengthened my knowing.

As I prepared to go for a long walk I felt a sense of dread. This surprised me because I love walking for exercise. When I checked in with myself I remembered this was the day I walk an intense hill. When I say intense, that's putting it mildly. This thing has me breathing hard and legs burning the minute I turn the corner to start the climb. Some days it feels like a mountain.

Realizing the negative story I was telling myself about this hill, I put a stop to it immediately. I told myself that I would climb the hill with ease. I imagined walking up it swiftly and joyfully. After a few minutes my whole energy shifted and I was actually looking forward to the hill for the first time ever.

Guess what happened? Yep. I walked up that hill with more ease and strength than I have in the four months I've been walking it. I didn't even drink the water that I normally almost finish before I get to the top. I had energy to spare, and for the first time, I was able to fully take in, and enjoy, the magnificent view that awaits anyone who climbs this beast. I share this with you because even after years of paying attention to any negative stories I tell myself, there are times I fall short.

Notice what stories you tell yourself when you're having difficulty accomplishing or changing something in your life. It requires regular practice to become aware of your Gremlin stories. And like anything else you want to master in life, it's always worth the practice!

RELEASING BOREDOM

$\sim$

I received a call from a friend telling me how bored she was. "There's nothing to do. I'm done with my work and no one's around! I'm going nuts, come over and hang out." I couldn't. And because I know how antsy she gets when there's 'nothing to do' I suggested that she relax and really enjoy this down time. Relish the peace and ability to just BE (Boredom Eliminated).

Although she wasn't too keen on the idea, she got my point since she's usually running all over the place and agreed to give it her best effort to relax.

Boredom is one of those sneaky little Gremlin moments that can keep you from connecting with yourself at a deeper level. I know it sounds crazy, but there is no reason in the world to be bored even when you're just staring at four walls. Those are the opportunities that allow you to look inside and grow spiritually and emotionally.

In a world where it appears that the busier you are, the more important your life is, it's easy to become disconnected to what's really true for you. And the minute there's enough room to feel what that is, it can unconsciously have you busying yourself once again when you're uncomfortable with your new awareness.

Boredom keeps you from feeling and noticing every moment of your life and appreciating all of it. Yes, even the painful stuff.

Because in those painful feelings are opportunities for learning and growth.

So the next time you're bored, use it as a gift to learn more about yourself. Oh yeah, my friend? She called and said she had one of the best afternoons of her life 'doing nothing' and couldn't wait to be bored again!

THE DREADED STORY

Sometimes it's easier to hold on to an unpleasant experience and retell it many times than it is to let it go and never bring it up again.

A friend of mine had just come back from a wedding in which she was a bridesmaid. The experience for her was less than pleasant, to say the least. Listening to her story, I couldn't help but think how much she was enjoying telling me the miserable details just so she could relive it all over again and play the role of victim.

As she continued, I realized that she had actually gotten through the experience quite nicely and took the high road in many ways. I pointed this out to her but she brushed it off and kept focusing on the difficulties.

Here's the deal, when you've had an experience that wasn't enjoyable, the bottom line is this; you made it through! And when you continue telling the story only to describe every lousy experience, you keep yourself in that lower energy. You deny yourself the opportunity to recognize what you learned, how you grew from it, or that you actually handled yourself quite well considering the circumstances.

CHANGING THE WORLD OR CHANGING YOUR PERSPECTIVE?

I believe we live in a world of more goodness than not. Why? Because of the people I meet everyday that want to make a difference in the world — who want to change the world for the betterment of humanity. I commend these people.

And, I also believe that sometimes there's an easier way to change some things in the world by changing our perspective. Doing this allows us to have a different experience, and then maybe, we won't feel the need to change what we originally thought needed changing. Changing our perspective can be the difference between living with frustration or living with joy.

Here are some questions to consider, where a change in perspective just might change your whole world:

1. Are you struggling with money because your job doesn't pay enough or because you spend too much?

2. Do you struggle with relationships because people don't understand you or you find fault with others easily?

3. Do you need a bigger place to live or do you have too much junk?

4. Is it difficult to loose weight or do you eat anything you want to and not exercise?

Think about it. When you come up with an honest answer you'll know what to do.

IF ONLY...THEN I...

If only... Then I... Four little words that can have such a profound effect in the way we create our life.

> If only he wouldn't be so angry all the time.
> If only she would be more patient.
> If only they were more appreciative at work.
> If only my job paid more.
> If only I had more time.
> Then I...(you fill in the blank).

When you find yourself saying, "If only" and "Then I" — you give away your power to someone or something outside of you. Any time you focus on the external and everything that's not working with it, you are destined to keep it as is.

So notice when you say, "If only...Then I" and change it to, "What if I..."

These three words not only open you up to new possibilities and ideas for circumstances to be better, it shifts the power back to you completely. And it's the internal power that gives you the ability to live a life that's free of, "If only... Then I..."

HAVE TO OR GET TO

So often when we change even just one of our spoken words we can literally shift our energy at the same time. Changing from "I have to..." to "I get to..." can set you up for a better experience with whatever it is you're going to be doing.

"I have to" can lower your vibration and diminish your personal power. Take a moment with each sentence below and notice if you feel any different when saying, "have to" then "get to."

I have to go to work.
I am fortunate to have a job and get to go to work.

I have to pick up my child from school.
I am grateful I'm home for my child and that I get to pick her up from school.

I have to visit my mother.
I appreciate what my mother has done for me and that I get to visit her.

I have to exercise.
I am grateful for my health body and that I get to exercise to keep it healthy.

I have to meet with a client.
I have my own wonderful business and I get to meet with another client.

I have to save money.

I appreciate earning money and I get to save it for special occasions.

I have to make dinner.

I am blessed to have this food and get to make dinner for my family.

I have to find a new job.

I am grateful I have marketable skills and get to find a new job.

I have to lose weight.

I love myself exactly as I am and I get to lose weight, too.

Play with replacing "have to" with "get to" with circumstances in your life, and see what difference it makes for you in your day-to-day experiences and energy.

LOVING THE MYSTERY, NOT THE HISTORY

I would love to take credit for this title and the idea behind this particular writing, but I can't. I heard these words spoken by Rev. Michael Beckwith while attending one of his services at Agape. When I heard them, they resonated so deeply with me I knew I would write about it.

I realize that one of the scariest things for people is the unknown, which in fact is a mystery. So the idea of loving the mystery is a stretch for many people, and if you're one of those people, then I invite you to consider this.

When you start to release your history, no longer attached to what was, and move into the mystery of your life that is unfolding, amazing possibilities are already forming. They're already there waiting to reveal themselves to you in their physical form and you actually help speed up the process as you let yourself love the mystery, not the history.

When you stop being more invested in what you've already accomplished or any tragedy you survived, wearing it like a badge of honor, you will find yourself attracting to you new opportunities to keep you expanding and growing beyond anything in your history.

So go for it! Start loving the mystery and not the history!

THE WIND IS BLOWING
IN THE WRONG DIRECTION

That was said to me by a woman I passed by during my walk. Actually, her exact words were, "This is terrible! The wind is blowing in the wrong direction."

It's fascinating to me how our filter system can have us viewing our circumstances as good or bad. I was walking in the same wind direction as she was and all I thought to myself, prior to passing this woman, was how invigorating it is having the wind in my face and making my walk harder, allowing me to work my muscles even more as I tackled the hill.

I loved it! She hated it! Two completely different experiences in the same environment.

She chose to tell herself a story that had her struggling with the environment. As far as I could tell, the wind wasn't stopping any time soon and no matter how much she hated it, she was going to have to deal with it. I so wanted to go back to her and share my perspective but I figured she'd think I was nuts. And besides, who am I to think she should have a different experience than the one she was going through!

So I continued on my way feeling grateful for the ability to be able to move through a challenging walk and allowing the wind to just be, no matter what direction it was blowing!

I encourage you to pay attention to the stories you tell yourself that cause you struggle and see how you can turn them around so you find a way to embrace the experience and ease the struggle.

CHAPTER 6

LAW OF ATTRACTION

AN INVITATION
FOR YOUR LIFE

Everything in the universe is made up of build-
ing blocks in the form of energy. Quite literally we are all One
and energy is actually a vibration, which means, everything that
exists in the universe vibrates, including us!

It's important to know, even though energy vibrates, there are
different levels of vibrations. Just like with musical instruments.
The difference though, is musical instruments are fairly consistent
with their vibrations while we're all over the place with ours. We
send out a ripple effect of highly charged emotional energy that
the universe picks up on, eventually sending back to us a dose
of similar energy that becomes our personal reality.

Whether you realize it or not, every single day you send out
an invitation for your life, through your vibration, addressed to
the universe. Now the universe, unlike many people who receive
an invitation, always sends you an RSVP. The good news is that
when you're clear about your invitation, created in the highest
vibration possible, and you remain in this vibration, your RSVP
can come quickly, easily and effortlessly, leaving you thrilled
with who and what shows up at your party of life.

The problem, however, is far too many people don't experience this for themselves and many aren't even aware that they
send out this invitation every day.

If you *are* aware, but you're not receiving the RSVP that you intended, it's because once that invitation is out there, your Gremlin shows up and gives you all sorts of reasons why the people or situations you invited can't come to your party. And guess what? You believe it.

On the other hand, when you're not aware of sending out the invitation, your Gremlin plays a part in this too. It's busy inviting all sorts of people and things into your life on your behalf that keeps it in power while you remain asleep to the invitations of the Gremlin. This is also known as a surprise party!

Maybe your surprise party has people who constantly take advantage of you. It's not what you want, but nonetheless, they keep showing up. As you keep moaning and groaning about these people, your Gremlin feeds on that lower vibration. It will make sure it continues since the universe delivers to you what you give your attention to. And that in turn, gives your Gremlin the power to remain the host of the party.

If you're not particularly fond of surprise parties, then it's up to you to gently and lovingly wake yourself up and send out your own invitations with the help of your Genie — invitations that hold a higher vibration.

Once you've sent out the invitations, then it's important to not let your consciousness go to sleep while the Gremlin takes over. Don't let your Gremlin deceive you into thinking your work has been done.

As you stay alert and conscious to all the invitations for your life, the next time you open the door to greet your guests, you'll find yourself embracing them with great love and appreciation for coming to your party since it's exactly who and what you wanted!

Stand Up and Stretch

One of the things I love most about working with my coaching clients is watching what happens when they're finally willing to stretch outside their comfort zone.

It could take days, weeks, or even months of encouragement and guidance as I watch them build their confidence before they say yes when asked to stretch beyond their preconceived limitations around a certain issue. However, what's so beautiful to be a part of is what happens when they finally take that leap.

They end up flying higher than they ever imagined possible. They discover that they're stronger and more capable than they ever realized before. And, even more exciting, is when they experience the support that shows up from the universe as they expand beyond their comfort zone.

When you're willing to stretch, you begin building an inner trust that things really can change and be better. No one can stretch for you. They can support you, but you've got to do the physical and mental work yourself.

So, what can you do that will allow you to stand up and stretch? Here's some ideas:

1. If you never apologize first after an argument, do so the next time.

2. Ask for the raise you keep being promised, but don't receive.

3. Create boundaries for yourself with others where there are none.

4. Join Toastmasters if you dream of speaking professionally but are afraid.

The key is to not judge the size of the stretch, just allow yourself to feel uncomfortable enough to not want to do it, but you're still willing to go for it — because in your heart, you know it will move you to a new level emotionally and spiritually.

If your Gremlin is showing up big time, it's probably a good stretch! Review the 5 tips to quiet it down and stretch away.

1. **Let your Gremlin be when it starts up with you.** Focus more on your body and see where it's showing up in your body. Does your head hurt? Is your neck stiff? Is your stomach in a knot? Breathe into those areas until you feel some relief.

2. **Give your Gremlin permission to rant and rave for a bit.** Don't judge it, don't panic over what's being said or resist anything. Just let it be. Allow all the Gremlin's ranting to pour out. Sit back and enjoy it for a change. Put a smile on your face as you listen calmly. Separate yourself from that Gremlin who's doing all the whining and complaining.

3. **Ask it questions. Get as intimate as you can with it.** Find out what sets it off. Then give it answers like you were talking to a four year old trying to calm her of the dark before falling asleep.

4. **Pick a name for your Gremlin and talk to it out loud.** Using its name, tell it everything is going to be fine and it can take a rest for now. Keep talking to it until it's less noisy. Talking out loud will create a shift

inside of you that won't happen when you just think about the conversation.

5. **Be gentle with your Gremlin.** Visualize your arm around it, soothing it, comforting it, allowing it to rest its head on your shoulder. Remember, it's scared, it doesn't want you to fall down and it believes it's doing what's best for you.

You can download these 5 tips off my website and put them in a place you'll see them every day as a regular reminder. *www. awakenthegeniewithin.com*

THE GIFT OF SURRENDERING

One of the greatest gifts we can give ourselves is the ability to surrender. The problem for many people however, when it comes to surrendering, is they have a belief that they're giving up, when in truth, just the opposite is happening.

Surrendering means you're letting go and releasing to a higher power. When you've done everything you can do on your end and have run out of ideas, surrendering is the next best step. Surrender to no longer forcing an outcome. Surrender to not knowing how the money is going to appear. Surrender to not needing others to agree with you and trust your own instincts. And surrender your time frame to the universe's time frame.

A girlfriend of mine had been out of work for a year and needless to say she was going through an extremely difficult time financially and emotionally. When she went to pay her mortgage she was shocked to discover that there was much less in her bank account than she thought. In that moment she lowered her head and said, "That's it. I surrender. I've done everything I know to get work. I'm turning it all over to you, right now."

She told me a great sense of peace washed over her when she did this. She knew, in that moment, she had truly surrendered for the first time in a year. What's remarkable is what happened fifteen minutes after she surrendered with those words. The phone rang and the person on the other end was requesting she come in for a job interview. This was a job she had applied for many months ago and hadn't heard anything. A little while later the phone rang again. It was for another job interview with another company she applied to. Within an hour, she received two job interviews. Within one week, she was working full time and still is. She's extremely grateful and looking for more wonderful opportunities to continue to unfold in her life.

When you're holding onto a lot of negative emotions that keep your energy at a lower vibration, surrendering frees you up to raise your vibration and attract new circumstances and ideas that are a better match for you. The next time you find yourself struggling and are full of worry and fear, hand it over to the universe and go do something nice for yourself!

THE F WORD
ELIMINATES STRESS

A t a certain time in my life I was in an emotional place that I hadn't experienced in a long time. Stressed!

There were many things I was working on personally and professionally which were all very exciting. So why the stress? Because I had been ignoring one key component that always keeps my stress level down.

The F word! Oh c'mon. You should know me better than that by now. Not *that* F word! The other F word!

FUN!!!!

I forgot to include fun in my day. And when I'm not having fun then not only does my work suffer, but my personal life suffers and my physical Being suffers. So you know what I did?

Of course you do! I dropped everything and had some fun. And you know what else? It worked wonders. So here's the deal. I don't care how much you've got going on in your life. I don't care how overwhelmed you are emotionally with problems in your life. You abSOULutely must make it a practice to keep fun alive in your daily life.

It doesn't matter how big or little the fun is. It only matters that you're doing something that puts a smile on your face, gives you a belly laugh, and when you think back on it, you feel really good inside!

Five reasons why having fun is so big:

1. It awakens your Genie within.

2. It allows you to manage your emotions.

3. It attracts to you more of what you want.

4. It reconnects you with your soul who's been begging for fun.

5. It quiets that annoying Gremlin.

How many more reasons do you need? Now get out there and have some fun!

CNN in the Bank

Is my bank the only bank that does this? Shows a running program of CNN on three big flat screen TVs that are up high behind the tellers. While the customers wait in line they're bombarded with nothing but one disaster after another that's happening around the world.

When I looked at everyone in line all I saw were people completely engrossed in what they were watching and looking very serious. No smiles, no one talking to anyone, and one woman actually had tears in her eyes as she watched. Unfortunately, they weren't even aware of what they were allowing into their consciousness.

If your bank does this I encourage you to not pay attention to the screen in front of you. We are bombarded with more negative information than positive every day of our lives thanks to the various forms of the media. This makes it so much more difficult to keep our energy up and our thoughts in a place that serves our highest good when we're exposed to situations like the one at my bank.

If you want to attract a wonderful life for yourself then it's up to you to make a conscious effort to keep your thoughts and feelings in a place that allow you to feel as good as possible every single day. Doing this allows you to be an open vessel to receive all the good that is sitting outside your door just waiting for that one opening so it can come in!

Maybe I'll suggest showing the cartoon network next time I'm in my bank!

What *is* Working?

I'd like to invite you to do one thing for an entire day. Focus on everything that is working throughout your day. I'm serious. No matter what yucky stuff happens, immediately search the Genie part of your mind for something else that already worked in your day or is working in the moment.

Here's a secret to help you come up with something:

There's always something working! Even if it's as obvious as, "I'm breathing." "I have a car to get me from point A to B." "I've got enough money to pay for the bus or cab to get me from point A to B."

You see, we're so quick to dismiss the everyday stuff, that we often forget how much *is* working in our life. I know it sounds trite, but until you start changing your thought pattern when you feel like your life isn't working the way you want it to, your life will continue to be as it is.

And one more thing, notice how putting your focus on what *is* working, makes you feel!

I Don't Want...

I went to see a photography show and ended up standing in line for an hour to get in. Glad to say it was well worth the wait! Since I was alone, I decided to entertain myself and listen to the various conversations going on around me.

There were three words that were being spoken on a regular basis. Words that are used by many people in general: "I don't want."

Waiting in line I heard statements like:

"I don't want my mom to find out I lost the money."

"I don't want my co-worker taking advantage of me anymore."

"I don't want to struggle with this project, but it's really hard."

I would imagine they haven't got a clue that just saying those three little words will often bring them exactly what they don't want. Why? Because that's the Law. You see, the universe has no favorites. It doesn't read between the lines. It only knows that as you speak, you create a vibration and whatever that vibration is, the universe picks it up and goes about doing its job of bringing back to you a circumstance that matches your vibration.

The words, "I don't want" will create a lower vibration in you. It will bring you a lack of what you wish for. This is exactly how we create the life that exists for us over and over again.

So I remind you, pay attention to your words and notice how many times you express yourself with "I don't want." And when you hear yourself saying that, just switch over to "What I want is..."

The more you talk about what you want and the more you feel great about that want, the higher your vibration and then the universe can bring you a circumstance that matches that vibration which will be much more to your liking.

I DON'T KNOW HOW, BUT I PROMISE

I heard these words, "I don't know how, but I promise" while watching a special on TV. The statement resonated so strongly with me that it sent a surge through my body.

The fact that someone was willing to make a promise to another person to help make a lousy situation better without knowing how he could do it, was a beautiful example of caring, compassion, devotion and trust. There was such fire in him when he said these words that there was no question a solution would be found.

How many times in your life do you find yourself unwilling to make promises to yourself because you have no idea how you might make that promise a possibility and that possibility a reality? Knowing the how is not what matters most. Having the heart, belief, desire and trust in getting something done is what matters most. Taking the first step toward something that's important to you is what matters most.

Today, have the courage to make a promise to yourself just because you're important enough to make promises to. It doesn't have to be some big, monumental event. It can be something small. Something that you've been afraid to take a step toward for fear of not knowing how it could actually manifest. And as you do this, allow yourself the room to change course along the way until you fulfill your own promise.

WHAT IS IT YOU WANT TO CREATE?

So what *is* it you want to create for yourself? Whatever it is you must *Be* it first.

Do you want to create:

1. A loving relationship? Love yourself first and share that love with others.

2. A job you love? Appreciate the job you have now.

3. More respect from others? Respect yourself and show respect to others.

4. More money? Give what you can to a person or organization that means something to you.

5. Greater peace for yourself? Think peaceful thoughts and be peaceful with others.

6. More harmony with your family? Be the harmony first.

7. Acceptance from others? Stop judging others and accept yourself exactly as you are.

The more you become what it is you want to create; the more you will find yourself experiencing it. And what you continue to experience is based on four elements in your life; your thoughts, words, actions and feelings. When these elements are not in alignment with each other for your highest good, it's not uncommon to find yourself coming up short with what it is you want to create.

You can't fool the universe. It operates on energy. Start shifting your energy so it matches all that you intend to create for yourself.

THINKING VS. THINKING

Many years ago Harvard and Yale did a study revealing that the average person thinks over fifty thousand thoughts a day. No real surprise considering our minds can be an ongoing chatterbox. What *is* worth noting is they also mentioned that most of the thinking was negative.

So that got me thinking. I thought to myself, "Well, there's thinking and then there's THINKING." The thinking in lower case letters would be the limited thinking and the upper case letters represents the expansive THINKING.

Next time you're thinking, look more closely. Are you thinking the same thoughts over and over again that don't necessarily inspire you or give you an opportunity for growth? Are you thinking lower thoughts that fall into the mass consciousness?

Or, are you THINKING along the lines of the individual Divine Being that you are, giving you an outlet to a whole new world of possibilities and all that you can become?

THINK about it.

YOUR BEST YEAR EVER.
ARE YOU PREPARED?

So I'm just wondering. With each New Year that comes upon us, do you commit to making it your best year ever? You deserve to have your best year ever and with that said I have another question for you. Are you prepared? Now you may be thinking, "Of course I'm prepared! I know this is my year! I can just feel it!"

That's a great start. It's important to feel whatever it is you desire for yourself. And, here are a few more tips to help you be even more prepared:

1. Make sure your beliefs align with your desires.

2. Take actions that inspire you.

3. Pay attention to the words you speak.

4. Maintain your faith even when nothing seems to be happening.

5. Be willing to make new choices, even if they scare you, when those choices are for the better.

6. Think in ways that keep you connected to your inner Genie.

7. Allow yourself to see others and yourself as Divine Spiritual Beings.

8. Say no to anything that doesn't support your highest good.

9. Move on from people who hold you back.

10. Ask questions that can move you forward.

Yep, there's more to do than just *feeling* prepared. You've got to prepare yourself with all your heart and soul every day on many different levels. Because anything less than that may leave you coming up short of your best year ever. I wish you a joyous year, every year.

CHOOSING HAPPINESS

⟨decorative flourish⟩

The following story is a beautiful example of how you can make the Law of Attraction work in your favor.

The ninety two year old, petite, well-poised mother-in-law of my best friend, who is fully dressed each morning by eight o'clock, with her hair fashion-ably coiffed and make-up perfectly applied, even though she is legally blind, moved to a nursing home today.

Her husband of seventy years recently passed away, making the move necessary. Maurine Jones is the most lovely, gracious, dignified woman that I have ever had the pleasure of meeting. While I have never aspired to attain her depth of wisdom, I do pray that I will learn from her vast experience.

After many hours of waiting patiently in the lobby of the nursing home, she smiled sweetly when told her room was ready. As she maneuvered her walker to the elevator, I provided a visual description of her tiny room, including the eyelet sheets that had been hung on her window. "I love it!" she stated, with the enthusiasm of an eight-year old having just been presented with a new puppy.

"Mrs. Jones, you haven't even seen the room...just wait."

162

"That doesn't have anything to do with it," she replied. "Happiness is something you decide on ahead of time; whether I like my room or not doesn't depend on how furniture is arranged, it's how I arrange my mind. I already decided to love it. It's a decision I make every morning when I wake up. I have a choice: I can spend the day in bed recounting the difficulty I have with the parts of my body that no longer work, or get out of bed and be thankful for the ones that do.

"Each day is a gift, and as long as my eyes open, I'll focus on the new day and all the happy memories I've stored away...just for this time in my life. Old age is like a bank account...you withdraw from it what you've put in."

~ AUTHOR UNKNOWN

I leave you with this question: Who's making deposits into your bank account, your Genie or your Gremlin?